THE POTENT MAN

By
M MacFarlane

First published in Great Britain in 1993 by Carnell Limited, 37 Salisbury House, London Wall, London EC2M 5PJ.

Typeset by SJ Design and Publishing, Bromley, Kent.

Printed by Repro City Limited, London.

ISBN 1-85779-124-X

Preface

Books on a medical subject are often difficult to understand, so full of complex medical terminology that ordinary people have trouble reading them. Or they are written by experts in a particular field with years of experience who may bring their own biases as to the subject with which they are so familiar, into the pages of their books. As a medical writer, I understand the medical terminology and am in contact with a great variety of experts in many fields. I have spent countless hours in the research libraries, doing computer searches of the latest research published in this particular field, and poring over the journals and statistical analyses that usually accompany articles scientists write for an audience of their professional peers.

I have distilled that information and made it readable, interesting and clear, so that those who are concerned about the problems of impotency, the reclaiming or retention of potency, may have questions answered and be helped in the search for a solution.

This information is not intended as a substitute for the advice of a qualified physician, but hopefully it will encourage further enquiry and aid in making the decisions that can improve the quality of life.

TO THE READER

The information in this book is not intended to replace the advice of your physician. You should consult your physician concerning any medical condition which concerns you. The material presented in this book is intended to inform and educate the reader so that he/she might make some intelligent choices in pursuing treatment and help. Neither the author nor the publisher assumes any responsibility or liability for the judgements or decisions a reader might make as a result of reading the contents of this publication.

Table of Contents

Introduction

When I began this book, people often asked me about the nature of the project. Most of these people either knew me or knew of my background as a medical writer. When I told them that I was writing a book about impotence, the reactions surprised me. Instead of the usual questions, there was a sudden silence. Instead of the usual polite interest or mild curiosity, there was embarrassed laughter, often followed by jokes or ribald commentary. Men's faces went blank and they withdrew from the conversation.

After this happened several times, I tried altering the way in which I presented this information. It did not matter: no matter how I responded, the reaction was the same.

But – days, even weeks, later – these same men who had shown no interest, would often say something like this: "I don't have a problem myself, you understand, but I do have a friend (classmate, relative, colleague, associate) and I told him about your work. He said he'd be glad to look over your work and give you his viewpoint, if you would be interested."

It soon became abundantly clear that the topic of impotence makes most people feel very uncomfortable. It is, it would appear, the last taboo. It seems we can now talk about almost everything else that would have created discomfort and controversy not too long ago. Safe sex, abortion, incest and homosexuality, are only a few of the topics that are no longer forbidden.

Sexual identity is only a portion of each person's concept of self but it is an integral part. For women, that sexual part of self is not dependent on the performance of any of their body parts, although the appearance of or 'beauty' of these parts might be very important to them and their concept of who they are. But, of course, this is quite different for men. If a man cannot have or maintain an erection it is obvious to him and to his sexual partners that he has a 'problem', that he has a body part that is not 'working'. Male sexuality expert Bernie Zilbergeld wrote that a man is expected to have a penis that is 'two feet long, hard as steel, and able to perform all night'.

A man who has a problem with erections, in either getting one or maintaining one, is more than likely to feel both anxious and ashamed. Rather than risk being thought of as a failure he may avoid sex completely. The longer he goes without sexual, or physical contact, the more frightening it becomes for him to even think about attempting to perform and the more unlikely that he will confront the problem. Ultimately, he may lose the sense of himself. Researchers have written that men are penis-centred and that the penis is the location of the male soul. This is often not understood by women who dismiss it as an explanation for the sometimes undesirable behaviour they observe in some men. For some women, the concern men have about potency is unreasonable because they are never confronted by a similar problem of dysfunction. The extent of the problem of impotence is enormous. Perhaps one in twenty-five men is impotent in the long term and almost every man has been unable to perform at one time or another and found himself excruciatingly troubled by that fact.

At the end of a long illness, it is said, the patient knows more about the malady than the doctor. In the case of impotence that old saying may be terribly wrong. After a long period of chronic impotence, most men are aware – sometimes to the point of thinking of almost nothing else – that they are impotent. They may be knowledgeable about what doesn't help, but they may also be totally uninformed about why the problem exists and what they might be able to do about it.

The fact is that millions of men suffer silently for approximately 10 years before they will acknowledge the problem and seek medical attention. It is often only then that they discover their problem is not psychological, is not that they have fallen out of love with their partner or that they need only to reduce the stress in their lives. Times have changed, fortunately: not too many years ago they might have been told that such a diagnosis was probably correct. They might have been told to relax or to take a little holiday, or to get some rest.

Today, about 90 per cent of impotence problems can be traced to specific medical causes and most of those causes can be treated. A wide variety of treatment options are now available, ranging from drug therapy to surgery. Furthermore, 97 per cent of impotency's problems can be helped with medication, psychological support, or surgical intervention. The odds are good that almost every impotent man can get help.

Because of attitudes in our society about how men are supposed to behave, men seem to think that it is a shameful weakness to have to admit to having a problem, a problem which affects their masculinity. One of the cornerstones of the masculine stereotype is that a man absolutely has to be a MAN. If he admits to problems with impotence, he is at risk of being thought of as less than a man, a serious indictment in any culture. A man is supposed to be knowledgeable and experienced, expected to know how to have good sex, and to perform frequently.

The male suffering from impotence will often embark on a search for an answer that protects his male ego. Because impotence doesn't prevent men from working or going about their day-to-day business of earning a living, supporting their families, or participating in the life of their community, millions of men suffer in silence rather than admit the problem. For some admitting to sexual difficulties is so painful that they would rather give up sex altogether than face that dilemma. Others find it easier to blame it on their partners or go in search for a partner who will inspire the desire necessary for an erection. Almost none of these men seem to realise that the problem might be medical and therefore treatable, and that, in fact, impotency is understandable in a climate which rewards men for being strong, virile and silent. Unfortunately, a man who has trouble getting an erection even 10 per cent of the time may find that without quick treatment, he can become chronically impotent.

Men assume that impotence causes psychological pain only to them. But when impotence enters into a relationship the partner may suffer just as much as the man. When intercourse is impossible for months, sometimes years, both become increasingly frustrated, both physically and emotionally. Frustration is then followed by a variety of other emotions: guilt, anger and hostility and these emotions often result in additional problems such as migraines, backaches, colitis and other stress-related illnesses. These symptoms are caused not so much by the lack of sex as by the emotional deprivation that accompanies impotence because impotent men often withhold all expressions of affection, from hand-holding to hugs, for fear they'll eventually be expected to perform.

At an impotence support group, formed by a local clinic, individuals and couples discuss with others their experiences with the problem of impotence.

Cleo said, "I began feeling old, ugly, fat, very unattractive. I didn't know what was wrong." Cleo frowned as she spoke. "If Charlie didn't want to have sex with me, could I continue to see myself as a real woman?" Married to Charlie for 16 years, Cleo didn't know what to do. "I thought that if he didn't want to have sex with me, then he must no longer find me sexually attractive and must not love me. And if he didn't love me, I must not be a worthwhile person." She and Charlie hadn't been fighting, hadn't had any serious conflict she could pinpoint. Their friends considered their marriage enviable. They had always talked things through, had been able to agree on goals for their lives. They had similar interests and had done lots of things together. They enjoyed going out to dinner and to the cinema, visiting friends and participating in activities with their children. Now, they just seemed to be growing slowly and silently apart. Charlie was working longer hours and seemed to be drinking more. He often stopped for a drink or two after work and then came home late; too late and too tired to do much else but have a couple more drinks and then fall into bed exhausted. When they did spend time together, he seemed withdrawn, and increasingly depressed. Nothing Cleo said or did made any difference. But when they did go out to dinner, she found he was making an absolute fool of himself over the waitress.

"He flirted outrageously," said Cleo. "It was if he desperately needed a stranger's attention but he had no desire to get that same kind of attention from me. I worried that maybe he had found someone else, that he was having an affair with someone at work."

Cleo went so far as secretly to follow Charlie for several weeks, only to find that he didn't seem to be deviating from his work routine and was working late all the times he told her he was. Then she anguished over what she had done by following and spying on him, to have such mistrust for her husband of 16 years.

"Sometimes I would lie awake at night watching Charlie. If I would touch him, he would pull away from me even in his sleep." There were tears in Cleo's eyes now as she spoke again. "I was so lonely I could have died."

It was not until Charlie had an automobile accident which required surgery on his leg fracture that routine tests revealed something else. It was discovered that he had undiagnosed diabetes, the cause of his impotence. When the diabetes was treated Charlie was restored to full potency.

"Then, and only then, was he able to tell me how he had suffered and worried about the problem, all by himself," said Cleo.

Charlie says, "When it first started, I was working on a project that required a great deal of my attention. It would mean a big promotion if it worked and probably would limit my future if it didn't. I was grabbing a hurried lunch at my desk and thinking about the project every evening. I began justifying a couple of big drinks right after work in the evening and a few before dinner because I felt I needed to relax. Becoming impotent was a big surprise to me. Not that I had ever considered myself a stud or anything like that, I just never had a problem before. Cleo was understanding. After all, we had been married for quite a while, had a good relationship. We did a lot of things together, talked over most things, made decisions together. So when I said I was just tired and had probably been working too hard, we just went to sleep and that was that. Or so I thought."

When Charlie was unable to get or maintain an erection for several months, he found that his anxiety level would rise rapidly when it looked like he would be expected to make love to his Cleo.

"Cleo would be dressed up when I got home from work," Charlie says, shaking his head regretfully and taking Cleo's hand in his.

"I started staying up later than Cleo, saying I had work I had to finish before I could come to bed. I worried that she might have discussed the problem with her mother or with her girlfriend, Jennifer. I couldn't bear the thought that they might know about it."

Cleo had tears in her eyes as she spoke. "We said some terribly mean and hurtful things to each other. I finally asked Charlie what was wrong, afraid that he would tell me he had found someone else."

Charlie took her question badly, "I lashed out at her. I told her I had enough on my mind with the job and all. Then I was really mean. I complained about the weight she had put on recently. I told her I thought her stomach had gone all mushy, that she was letting herself go. That ended in a big row and Cleo went off to bed by herself. I slept in the spare room that night. It was a relief. By getting her that angry at me I was able to avoid any kind of intimacy. I sort of tucked that notion away in the back of my head: by fighting with her I could avoid the situation altogether. I guess I actually began to pick fights with her so that we could both go to bed angry and I could sleep in the spare room."

Charlie went on to say, "But really, I was getting frantic. When I heard other men talking, joking about guys who couldn't get it up anymore, you know, locker-room kind of stuff, I would wonder whether they knew, whether their remarks were aimed at me. There was no one I could talk to about it. I began looking at the advertisements in the back of sex magazines, looking to see if I could find anything that would help me. I even wondered if I might have cancer or something. It was driving me crazy and I didn't know where to turn. I even considered suicide."

Charlie hunched over and looked at the floor before he spoke again. Cleo watched him with a pained expression on her face.

"I was drinking and working long hours, ruining my health and my marriage and I knew it. If I hadn't had that accident and found out about the diabetes, who knows what might have happened?"

Charlie looked up at the concerned faces of the others in this support group. "And sometimes I still wonder, if I hadn't found a solution, where would I be now? Would I still be married to Cleo?"

Both of them agree that they have done some serious damage to their relationship and their marriage. In the seemingly endless fights, they said a lot of mean and hateful things in their anger. Things that still need repair if they are ever to mend their relationship. They have been working with a marriage counsellor, trying to keep their marriage intact.

Cliff had nodded in agreement a number of times as Charlie spoke. He spoke next. "Although my situation is very different from Charlie and Cleo's, I can understand some of what Charlie was thinking.

"The first time I was unable to get an erection," says Cliff, "it was with someone I hardly knew, just a girl I had met earlier in the evening in a pub. I thought that I probably had just had too much to drink.

"Then for a while everything was OK, until the next time and then a third and fourth time. Now I was seized with panic. I thought, 'What if it is all over for me?' I began to think about things I usually didn't think about at all. I realised I was getting older and hadn't given a moment's thought to the future, old age or to settling down.

"As a single man, I thought I had a reputation to uphold. I believed I was the envy of all my married friends, the men who had been with the same woman for years and years. I used to laugh at them, kid them about what a boring sex life it must be, the same woman all the time. What was I going to do if I couldn't continue to be the Don Juan I always thought I was? I began having crazy mood swings. I bought every raunchy magazine and X-rated video available, trying to stimulate myself, trying to make something happen.

"The guys at work had always waited for me to come and tell them my wild tales of the night before. Now, as I couldn't get an erection time after time, I would just use the plot of one of the X-rated films to tell them, only I said it was happening to me. They would slap me on the back and tell me how they envied me.

"Finally I saw a doctor." Cliff laughed. "When I was afraid to ask anybody to go home with me, when I was tired of thinking about it, I went and had a medical check-up. It took me quite a while to get up the courage to go to the doctor. I was afraid he would laugh at me, or just dismiss the problem, because it wasn't life-threatening, or worse yet; I was afraid he might tell me it was all in my head."

Cliff laughed again, "The funny part of it was, that after the medical check-up, and he did all the tests, everything he could think of, and he couldn't find anything physically wrong, he did tell me that it was psychological.

"Once I knew that I didn't have any physical reason for the impotence, I was tremendously relieved. Now I knew, I thought it would just go away, but it didn't. Knowing that it wasn't physical didn't change anything.

"I took some of the doctor's advice. I cut back on my drinking and I stopped smoking, difficult as that was. I tried to be more reasonable in my eating habits and I stayed home a couple of nights a week, just watching TV and going to bed early.

"Now my nightmare was even worse as there didn't seem to be any reason for it that I could see. I didn't have any terrible disease or anything, but now I saw that I would have to work on the things that were bothering me, and I couldn't decide what those things could be. I have had to decide just what the things are that are stressful in my life, and if that is what is keeping me from getting erections. And that is one of the reasons I'm here in this group, to talk about that stress.

"The doctor referred me to a therapist who is helping me examine my basic beliefs about myself." Cliff shook his head forlornly, "I guess I am really just a normal kind of a guy, not the wild and crazy party animal that I like to think I am. I guess that has just been a pose. I've discovered that as I begin to reach middle age, I am finding that I really envy my friends who have long-term marriages and a bunch of kids. I have always been so afraid that if I get married I will get tired of a wife quickly and be stuck in a relationship I don't really want."

Charlie spoke quickly, "What you are saying, Cliff, is that you haven't wanted responsibility. You have wanted only relationships that were just for fun."

Cliff nodded his head in agreement, "That's right. Now I am slowly beginning to realise that my lifestyle was in conflict with my basic value system and without my knowing it, that was creating a tremendous amount of unconscious stress for me. Always looking for a one-night-stand, one where there would be no strings attached, one where we would both know it was just for fun, is a responsibility in itself. This kind of thinking hasn't been very easy for me. I've never been one to think about why I do something, I just do it. But now I'm working on it. When I was a kid my mother used to take us to church two or three times a week and I always said I had had enough of that stuff. One of the things I have done that I still haven't been able to tell the guys at work yet, is I've started going to church again. But now, when I am in such a turmoil, it seems very familiar and comforting to me. I really don't know, maybe it will help. I hope so. One thing I do know, I have no real physical reason for my impotence and I intend to keep working on it until I solve the problem."

Two very different case histories, two very different men, two very different sources of impotence. But both men can regain their potency and have happy and fulfilling lives. First, each man needed to go for a medical evaluation of his condition. Each man is now having to make some changes in the way he lives.

Charlie's changes are dietary because of the diabetes and with his wife's help, he has made those changes. He admits they aren't easy and he has to learn a lot about what he eats and how he eats but he has already found out a lot about his diabetes and how to control it. Now he has to work on his relationship with Cleo.

Cliff's changes are psychological. Although nothing is medically wrong with him, he is still impotent. He has to work out just where he wants his life to go and how he wants to live it. Until he resolves what has become for him a tremendous inner conflict, it will burden him with unmanageable stress and manifest itself in this most intimate area of his life.

DEDICATION

To the memory of:
MAY YOUNG KERR JOHNSTONE
Who taught me that
Knowledge is the antidote to fear.
Emerson, Society and Solitude: Courage (1870)

1 How Do Erections Work?

There is widespread ignorance about the workings of the penis; myths about it abound worldwide. "There is no organ," wrote Masters and Johnson in 'Human Sexual Response', "about which more misinformation has been perpetrated ... in art, literature and legend throughout the centuries."

It is unfortunate that most men have had their education about the penis, its anatomy and its functioning, from the locker-room. Ignorant little boys have whispered together and passed on tales and stories they heard from other boys. Nowhere has there been a book, outside of complicated technical physiology texts, that a boy could read and understand the true working of this organ which is controlled by the mind, and thought by some to be the centre of a man's soul.

To early man, the erect penis was a thing of mystery. Having absolutely no knowledge of anatomy, a connection between all kinds of magic and the erection was assumed.

Eastern philosophies believed there was a connection between breathing and sex and in various yoga disciplines breath control was of utmost importance. The philosophy of the East was that breathing stimulated something located at the base of the spinal cord; yogis spent a lifetime learning to control this life force.

Hippocrates, the Greek father of medicine, attributed the inability to maintain an erection to a preoccupation with business or an unattractive wife, opinions that linger to this day. In the Middle Ages it was thought that some kind of substance, perhaps a gas or a liquid of some kind, transmitted heat to the genital area and that heat caused the penis to swell.

The Greeks were possibly the first who began to see some type of mechanical connection in the process of the erection.

They observed that the testicles were lowered and went higher into the body recesses at certain times and they wondered if the testicles were meant to be counterweights, raising the penis as they lowered. What caused the testicles to raise or lower so that an erection might occur was not something they were able to comprehend.

To some degree, all of these ideas had substance: there is indeed some magic connected to the erective process, in that it is certainly a mystery to know or understand just what it is that arouses desire in each man. To one man, it is a beautiful blonde walking gracefully past him in the street. To another, it might be the connection to the scent of a particular flower. To yet another it might be the slight sheen of perspiration on his loved one's upper lip as they work together in the fields. It might be the curve of an upraised arm or the sound of a special voice calling his name.

And the connection between sex and breathing is logical since the arousal process increases not only the heartbeat but the rate of respiration.

The thinking of the early Greeks that the penis was mechanical was on the right track, if they had only realised that the penis is similar to other hydraulic devices. Just like a water balloon, which increases in both size and firmness when filled with water, there must be a way to keep it filled and to empty it when necessary.

An erection takes place when the penis is filled with blood. That blood must then remain in the penis long enough for intercourse to take place.

But in order for that to happen, there are three conditions required:

1. There must be the ability to relax the smooth-muscle tissue in the penis.
2. There must be an unobstructed supply of arterial blood into the erectile chambers.
3. There must be a blood-storage mechanism that will keep the blood within the erectile chambers until orgasm has taken place.

Lacking any of these conditions, a man will be unable to get or maintain a firm erection.

What Happens In The Brain Before The Physical Changes Of Arousal And Erection Occur?

The limbic system is a primitive part of the brain that controls bodily reflexes. It responds to such sensory input as odours, sounds and sexual signals from a desirable person. This limbic system is the animal in all of us; it was one of the first parts of the brain to evolve and controls such reflexes as thirst, hunger, fear and sexual arousal. These almost automatic responses to the senses are then reviewed by the more sophisticated parts of the brain, those which have been programmed by the culture, the attitudes of the society in which the individual lives and by the learning he has been given about the meaning of these sensations. These include a review by the moral code and conscience before allowing the primitive brain to respond. If the monitoring of the more sophisticated part of the brain gives the go-ahead, then the primitive centre is allowed to send electrical signals down the spinal cord, allowing the nerves throughout the body to respond appropriately to the stimuli.

What Happens Physically To The Body At The Time Of Arousal?

When the messages from the brain begin the arousal process, an increased volume of blood begins to flow throughout the body, causing the sexual organs to swell. Blood begins to pool in certain organs, the man's penis, the woman's clitoris and the breasts, which increase in volume by about 20 per cent. Small muscles contract at the base of the nipples, causing them to protrude. The skin at the stomach and buttocks cools, as well as at the fingers and toes, and the skin over the chest and breasts grows warmer; the sexual organs increase in temperature several degrees, all this taking place as the blood is diverted from areas which have less need for it at the moment than the sex organs. Blood is diverted to the muscles necessary for intercourse and the heart must pump faster to meet the additional circulatory needs of the sex act.

There is an increase in tension of all the muscles of the body and these working muscles, particularly those of the thighs and buttocks, need additional oxygen. The respirations increase, as well as the heart rate, which rises from approximately 70 beats per minute to about 180 beats a minute at orgasm, as the heart works to supply the additional oxygen and increased blood flow necessary.

The act of intercourse causes profound changes in blood hormone levels of familiar hormones such as testosterone and oxytocin. In addition, there is a release of a variety of hormones and chemicals which are not completely understood and are currently under study.

Finally, the pain threshold increases dramatically, caused by the release of endorphins, the body's natural pain killers, at the site in the brain which is responsible for the response to orgasm.

What Do The Body's Two Different Nervous Systems Have To Do With Erections?

The body's nervous system is divided into two main systems, the *central nervous system* (the brain and the spinal cord) and the *peripheral nervous system* (the one that sends signals between the central system and other parts of the body).

The peripheral nervous system is further divided. One section of it is the *autonomic nervous system*, which deals with such 'automatic' functions of the body as digestion and heartbeat.

One more division: the autonomic nervous system is further divided into the *sympathetic* and the *parasympathetic* systems. These two systems operate to balance one another, and are controlled by the emotions.

In arousal, the sympathetic system is in operation, causing the penis to be erect. When the penis is becoming soft again, during periods of calm, the parasympathetic system is in control.

After an orgasm, the autonomic nervous system becomes indifferent to the stimuli of sexual thoughts and stops flooding the erectile tissue with blood. The veins then catch up on their drainage work, and within minutes the penis is relaxed again.

No one yet fully understands the neurological shunts that direct all that extra blood into the erectile tissue when the aroused nervous system commands it to do so. Physically, it is possible to maintain a healthy erection almost indefinitely. Practically, the difficulty is keeping the autonomic nervous system stimulated for an indefinite period of time. The limits are more mental than physical.

Men differ widely in how long it takes to achieve another erection after an orgasm. The autonomic nervous system generally needs to go through a 'refractory phase' (or rest period) before it can become reactivated. A 30-minute pause is normal for most men.

How Is An Erection Similar To A Hydraulic System?

An erect penis is one in which the total volume of a liquid in a low-pressure system has been increased to the capacity of that system. The system then has become a higher-pressure system and it expands until the surrounding tissue limits its expansion and becomes firm.

In order for this system to work there needs to be a high pressure supply of that liquid (in this case, blood), which is supplied by the arteries; an overcoming of the parasympathetic nervous system by the sympathetic nervous system (the nerves which send an 'erect' message as opposed to a 'soft' message); and a storage mechanism that will maintain the liquid in the system (blood kept in the penis by the compression of the veins, which, for the period of intercourse, does not allow it to recirculate).

Figure 1 is a cross-section of the male pelvic organs; below are some simple explanations of their various functions.

Figure 2 is a cross-section of the penis; below are explanations of the functions of the various chambers.

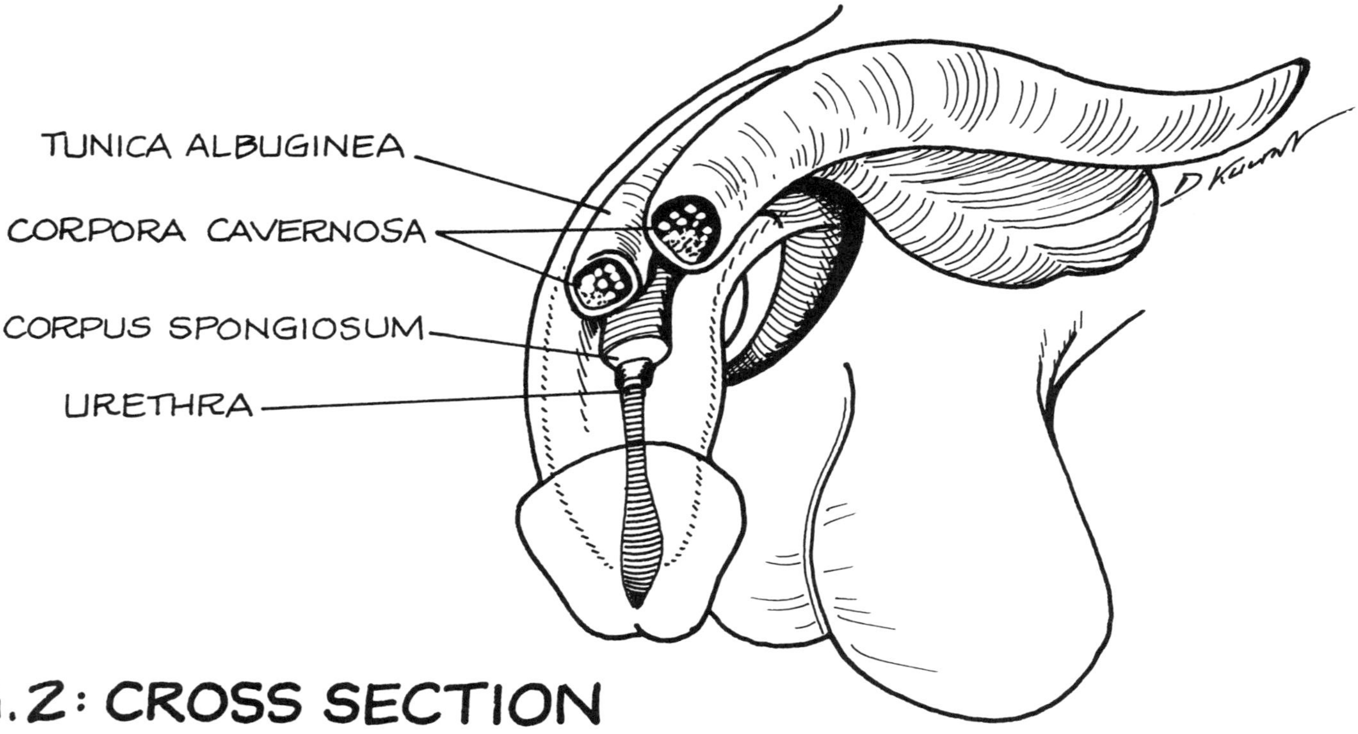

FIG. 2: CROSS SECTION OF THE PENIS

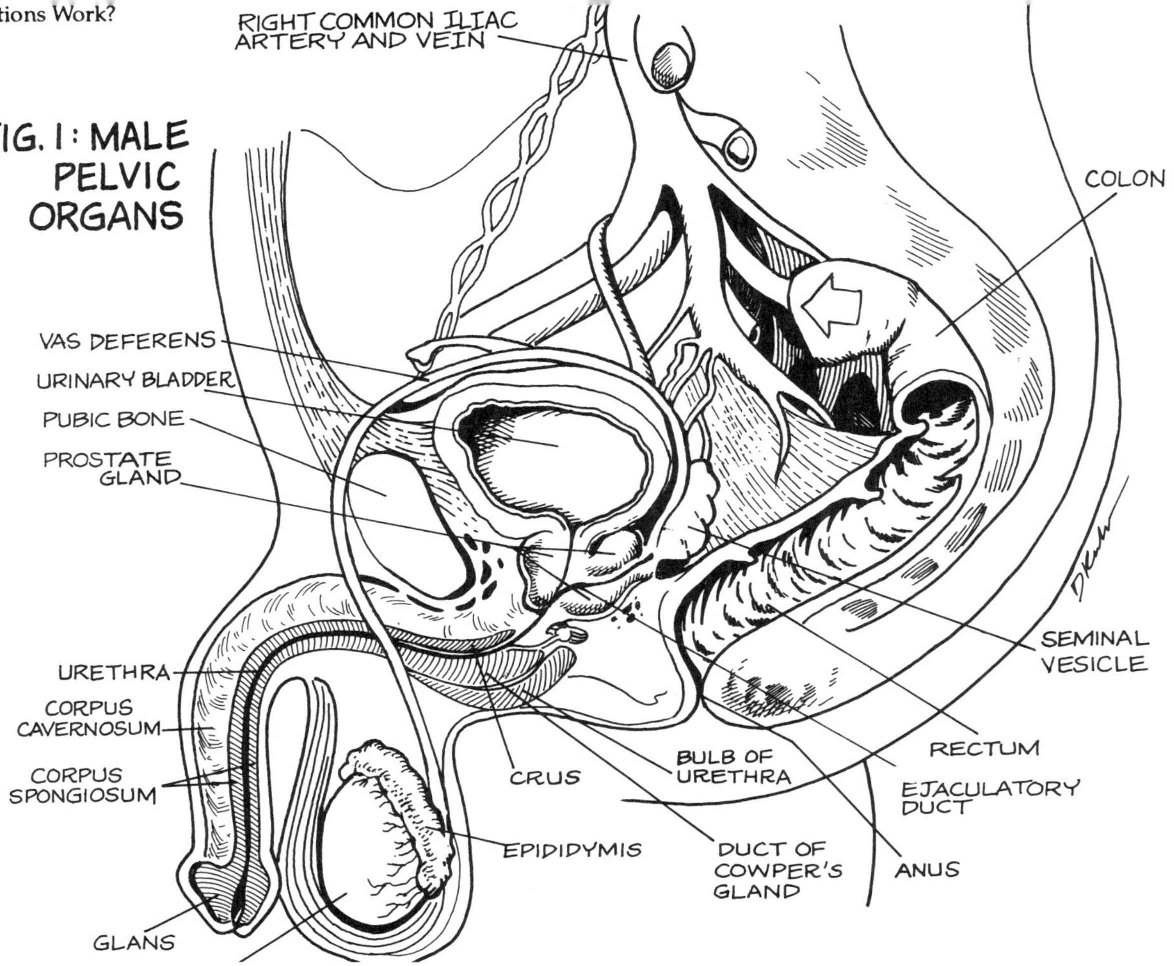

FIG. 1: MALE PELVIC ORGANS

What Is The Main Function Of The Testicles?

The testis, or testicle, is an egg-shaped gland, situated in the scrotum, which produces sperm. Testicles vary in size from that of hazelnuts to large chicken eggs. The testicles are filled with yards and yards of micro-thin tubing. It is within this tubing that the sperm are produced and then stored. Between these micro-thin tubes are small areas where 95 per cent of the male hormone testosterone is produced (a very small additional amount is also produced by the adrenal glands). The function of testosterone is the induction and maintenance of male secondary sex characteristics.

Normally, testicles are about 1¼ to 2 inches long and half an inch wide. In most men the left testicle hangs lower and is a little bit smaller than the right. They are surrounded by a protective sack of skin and involuntary muscle known as the scrotum. The creasteric muscle encloses the connection of each testicle to the body. These muscles keep the testicles close to the body and assist in the regulation of internal temperature. Sperm is produced at a temperature a couple of degrees lower than the rest of the body and these muscles relax and contract, allowing the testicles to be lower in warmer weather and closer to the body when the weather is cold.

The testosterone produced here initiates the libido and influences the ability to have an erection. However, small babies are able to have erections and prepubescent boys, who have very little testosterone, have erections, so the connection between the effect of testosterone and erections is still unclear.

Differences in testicle size from species to species appear to be related to the demands that are placed on them to produce sperm and are largely due to the differences in the number and length of the sperm-producing micro-tubing.

In comparing body weight to testicle size, man's testicles are 0.079 per cent of total body weight, while a chimpanzee's testicles comprise 0.269 per cent of its total body weight. Within our own species size is usually a hereditary factor.

What Is The Raised Ridge Running Alongside Each Testicle?

The soft, raised ridge running alongside each testicle, just beneath the surface of the skin, is the epididymis. This oblong body is the place where new sperm matures.

What Do The Vasa Deferentia Do?

The testicles are suspended in the scrotal sac by a long cable called the spermatic cord. Within this cord, one on each side, lie the vasa deferentia. These narrow tubes convey sperm from each epididymis up through the pelvis into a wider part of the vas where sperm is stored.

Why Do Men Have A Prostate Gland?

Most of the bulk of semen is a protective medium, partially produced by the prostate gland. This protective medium enables sperm to survive the journey down the urethra and out through the penis. Only a small portion of semen is made up of sperm. The rest of it is seminal fluid and prostatic fluid.

When semen leaves the penis, it is actually a string of different fluids. First is the prostatic fluid, which is thin and watery, then the sperm from the testicles, followed by the fluid from the seminal vesicles, which is thicker. However, the prostatic fluid will contain a small amount of sperm. Almost immediately, at ejaculation, semen clumps due to a chemical reaction between the two secretions, seminal and prostatic. This chemical reaction produces a net of protein which forms to hold the sperm cells. After approximately 20 minutes at room temperature and more quickly in the warm environment of the vagina, the clump liquefies, releasing the sperm, which then swim into the cervix in search of an egg to fertilise, leaving the seminal fluid behind.

The functions of many of the secretions of the prostate gland are still unknown. One, spermine, is responsible for the odour of semen. Other chemicals liquefy the seminal clump after ejaculation, allowing the release of the sperm so they may travel to their destination, the ovum. Another is believed to be a natural antiseptic, killing potentially dangerous bacteria in the vagina which might harm the sperm, and others may stabilise the DNA, the genetic message carried by the sperm.

The prostate gland surrounds the neck of the bladder and the urethra. Upon ejaculation it contracts, assisting in expelling the mixture of sperm, seminal and prostatic fluids into the urethra and then out of the penis.

The prostate is approximately the size of a walnut and is totally dependent on testosterone for its growth and function. It has no effect on erection; its importance is in the production of prostatic fluid.

Does The Seminal Vesicle Produce Semen?

The seminal vesicle produces seminal fluid which, when mixed with the sperm from the testicles and prostatic fluid from the prostate gland, makes up the composition of semen. This pair of glands depend on hormones from the testicles for their activation.

How Important Is The Position Of The Bladder In The Male Pelvic Organs?

The bladder, which is a storage vessel for fluid secreted by the kidneys before it is discharged through the urethra, has nothing to do with male sexual function until it begins to be affected by the prostate gland later in life. Then, the pressure may cause difficulty in urination and cause the man to get up many times during the night, interrupting his sleep. It has no effect on the sexual functioning, only on the man's thoughts concerning it.

However, occasionally there are signals from a full bladder which can short-circuit the erection nerves, as the bladder nerves are parallel to the nerves which control erections.

By age 55 or 60, new prostatic tissue begins to develop. In its small space, this new growth presses upon the original gland, lifting the bladder into an unusual position and making it more difficult to empty completely.

How Does The Function Of The Urethra Differ In The Male And The Female?

In the female, the urethra is a canal conveying urine from the bladder to the outside and is only about $1^1/_2$ inches long. In the female that is its only function.

In the male this canal is approximately 8 to 9 inches long and has a dual purpose. It conveys urine from the bladder and also acts as a channel for semen during ejaculation. In a healthy man, urine and semen never enter the urethra at the same time.

What Is The Clear Liquid That Emerges From The Tip Of The Penis During Arousal?

This clear liquid, which is actually rather oily and thick, comes from the Cowper's glands, two small glands that sit in front of the prostate and are about the size and shape of a pea. It is believed that the exudate from these glands spreads down the tube in the penis which covers the inside of the urethra, neutralising any residual urine which might harm the live sperm and lubricating the urethra so that the sperm can move down it rapidly.

What Does 'Glans' Mean?

'Glans' is Latin for 'acorn', an obvious name for the end of the penis based on its appearance.

The glans is that part of the corpus spongiosum, or the spongy body, which surrounds the urethra and is the external portion of this, one of the three chambers of the penis. The two erectile chambers do not extend to this portion of the penis but end just at the ridge, the corona, which is at the base of the glans.

What Is The Corona?

At the base of the glans is a ridge, called the corona, which is Greek for crown. Immediately behind the corona, the skin of the penis extends outward and then folds back on itself, covering the glans. This hood, known as the foreskin, can be rolled back to expose the glans.

When a circumcision is performed, it is usually done right at the corona, removing the entire hood from this point on.

How Much Of The Penis Is Hidden?

One half of the human penis is actually inside the body of the male. It extends almost all the way to the anus, where it attaches to the underside of the pelvis. Between the anus and behind the testicles there is a hump and this concealed part of the penis is called the crus. The crus is vulnerable to injury and should be protected, particularly during active sports.

What Cushions The Urethra?

The corpus spongiosum (the name means 'spongy body') is one of three separate chambers within the penis but different in composition and function from the other two. It surrounds the urethra, lies underneath the other two chambers, and protects and cushions the urethra from injury, particularly from assaults occurring from beneath the body.

What Is The Purpose Of The Arteries In The Penis?

Arteries bring fresh oxygenated blood from the heart and lungs to every body part. They are thick, muscular vessels which can constrict and maintain a high pressure. The iliac artery brings blood to the lower half of the body. The corpora cavernosa arteries provide blood to the erection chambers.

During arousal, these arteries expand from 0.6 millimetres in diameter to nearly double that size, allowing this high-pressure arterial blood to fill the spaces in the two balloon-like chambers of the penis. Like a deflated balloon, these spaces then fill and expand, resulting in an erection.

What Is The Purpose Of The Veins In The Penis?

It is the job of the veins of the body to take the blood away from the body part where it was being used, return it to the heart and lungs for reoxygenisation and then, when no longer needed there, recirculation throughout the body.

Veins are thin-walled and able to expand and contract quite easily. Because they can so easily change their accommodation, they can drain blood back to the heart as quickly as needed.

During erection, the veins, which lie very close to the surface inside the two balloon-like structures, are squeezed almost shut by the filled erectile tissue pressing against the firm fibrous coating that surrounds these two chambers.

At this time, the blood return in them is reduced to a mere trickle. The blood which fills them can barely return, but when the penis is again flaccid, these veins reopen and take this blood rapidly back to the heart.

What Are The Two Balloons Of The Penis?

These two chambers, the corpora cavernosa, are the erectile chambers of the penis. They are two long balloon-like structures lying side by side. They are filled with tissue that consists of a microscopic sponge-like network of chambers known as lacunar spaces which are encased in elastic, densely fibrous tissue. When the penis is soft or flaccid, these spaces are flattened, just like empty balloons. During arousal, which is stimulated by sexual thoughts, they fill with blood which stiffens, lengthens and expands these separate chambers until the penis becomes erect and hard.

What Limits How Much These Two Balloon-like Chambers Will Expand?

The tunica albuginea (so named because it is a white tissue – literally 'white coat') tightly surrounds both of the large cylinders which are responsible for erection. This tough, fibrous tissue limits the amount of expansion possible. However, it is also quite flexible, allowing the penis to become shorter, longer, narrower or wider, depending upon that particular man's anatomical programming.

How Much Blood Does An Erect Penis Hold?

An erect penis holds approximately 8 to 10 times as much blood as that of a flaccid penis.

The blood pressure of a flaccid penis is approximately the same as that inside other low-pressure internal organs, such as the liver. Blood flows through the penis at the rate of about 0.3 ounces per minute. During arousal, that flow can reach a rate of four ounces per minute and the pressure in the penis rises dramatically, increasing by approximately 10 or 15 times. Once erection is achieved, blood flow in and out becomes balanced; an inflow of between $\frac{2}{3}$ of an ounce and $1\frac{1}{3}$ ounces per minute is necessary to sustain the erection. During an erection, the penis essentially becomes a separate, closed circulatory system with a blood pressure that is at least 10 times higher than the rest of the body.

What Is The Symphysis Pubis?

This is the place where the pubic bones join together at the centre of the body and are seen as a bony prominence directly beneath the pubic hair at the point where the penis emerges from the body.

What Is The Function Of The Foreskin?

At the tip of the penis is a dense mat of nerve endings that make it one of the most sensitive organs of the entire male body. The foreskin contains highly specialised glands that release an oily substance onto the head of the penis to prevent it from drying out and to protect it from both bacteria and fungus. It contains a complex biochemical apparatus that hormone researchers are still attempting to understand in its relationship to the male hormone testosterone.

The circumcised penis is subject to the abrading effects of clothing and the ammonia from urine. This can result in meatal stenosis, a hardening and narrowing of the urethral opening and a loss of the sensitivity of the head of the penis from the constant exposure to friction.

It is estimated that half of the males in the world have been circumcised. As a religious rite, circumcision can be traced back to the Egyptians. Some anthropologists believe that it was practised as far back as the Stone Age.

In the 1850s in the USA, the foreskin was blamed for a long list of medical disorders, from epilepsy to mental illness, and the medical textbooks of the times recommended removal for hygienic and health reasons. Two of the diseases it was said to affect were cancer of the penis and cancer of the cervix in women with whom the uncircumcised man had intercourse. This theory is now rapidly being disproven and current thinking is that the foreskin should be preserved and the male taught to retract the foreskin and frequently clean the smegma which collects there.

What Happens At The Time Of Ejaculation?

Just prior to reaching orgasm, men experience a sensation that they are about to ejaculate. This is because the sperm and fluids from the seminal vesicles have begun to fill a small chamber at the exit from the bladder.

The urethra, the tube from the bladder to the outside, has, at the exit from the bladder, two muscular valves, an inner valve and an outer valve, with a space between them. A reflex, triggered by sensory nerves around the penis, causes the sex glands to contract and the secretions from the various sexual organs, the prostate, the testicles and the seminal vesicles fill this space, which is a closed chamber. The nerves that control the opening and closing of the inner and outer valves of this chamber now close, creating a pressure chamber filled with the secretions from these glands. Once this pressure chamber is filled with semen, the walls of this chamber begin to stretch and sensory nerves located in those walls send a message to the brain that cause ejaculation. Now muscles at the base of the penis squeeze the pressure chamber by contracting at 0.8 second intervals. The muscles around the anus begin to contract spasmodically and at the same instant, the outer valve of this chamber relaxes for a fraction of a second and the muscles of the pelvic floor contract spasmodically causing the semen to be forced out under high pressure. This pressure is such that the seminal stream can reach distances of anywhere from six inches to a distance of three feet. Certainly far enough to guarantee that it will reach the cervix in order to deposit the living sperm within impregnating distance of the female's egg. At the same time, the egg is sending out chemical signals in order to guide and aid the sperm in locating it.

Anthropologists suspect that nature provides a protective mechanism in most species. To keep them safe from predators while copulating, male animals are programmed to ejaculate within a very short period after beginning intercourse. They are thus able to avoid deadly fights with other males aroused by the female in heat as well as predators attracted by the scent of the female who might find the male engaged in intercourse a distracted and easily accessible prey.

The human, on average, will ejaculate within two minutes after the start of intercourse. This time will vary only slightly, from between ten seconds to slightly more than three minutes.

As the male ages, he is able to delay ejaculation, partly because of the reduction of sensitivity of the penis and the slowing of various other muscle and nerve responses.

What Happens At The Time Of Orgasm?

Orgasm is associated with specific changes in the brain waves of the individual experiencing one. Bursts of electrical energy have been documented in experiments with monkeys when electrodes were implanted on a portion of the brain considered the pleasure centre.

During orgasm there are waves of activity in the sex glands as well as along the urethra. The nerves respond to the changes in pressure within the small chamber that holds the ejaculate as well as the pulsating contraction of the pelvic muscles as the ejaculate is expelled under high pressure. The muscles around the anus contract approximately once a second and the total body muscular tension which was present during intercourse is relaxed, bringing with it an intense feeling of relief and lassitude.

Experiments have shown that orgasm starts a few seconds prior to ejaculation in response to the muscular activity taking place in preparation for ejaculation. However, if ejaculation does not take place, the orgasm will not be as intense. When the internal valve on the pressure chamber is inefficient, the sensation is reduced because the tension in the pressure chamber is lowered. If the inside valve is either weak or damaged, the ejaculate will be retrograde, that is, into the bladder, and the muscle contractions of the urethra during orgasm will be weaker.

As it takes some time after ejaculation for these sex glands to refill the pressure chamber, men can experience a reduced orgasm after repeated ejaculation, simply because the sex glands are unable to refill the pressure chamber without a period of time for the response to take place. During foreplay, semen is produced during this excitement phase and the longer the period of foreplay, the larger the volume of semen, which contributes to the intense effect of the orgasm.

2 What Can Cause Impotence?

Impotence is defined as the inability to get or maintain an erection sufficiently hard for intercourse to ejaculation. If men would be truthful, most would admit that they have sustained an episode of impotence at one time or another of their lives. Although the causes for that first failure may be minor – fatigue, an unfamiliar situation, interruption by a crying child, any number of small things – it can be so devastating that a man's whole concept of his masculinity may be undermined.

Our society has taught men that they ought to be sexual at all times and able to get an erection on demand. If they cannot, they are total failures as men.

A second episode of impotence can create a climate of psychological uncertainty about a man's sexual future, leading to depression and a fear of failure that can become cyclical. But there is often a significant contributory cause, such as disease, drugs, a prescribed medication or an injury, and these need to be examined before any decision about the impotence is made. There are a number of causes of impotence beside the oft quoted "it's all in your head".

Because three things are necessary to get and maintain an erection (filling of the erectile chambers, smooth-muscle relaxation, and retention of blood in the penis long enough for orgasm), it is possible for some men to able to generate a semi-rigid erection while others might be unable to have any erection at all. Still others might be able to become erect but find that they are unable to maintain that erection.

Very few men find themselves able to have a good erection one day and then find that ability completely gone overnight. Most erectile problems occur over a period of time. Most men, after experiencing a few episodes of impotence or a period of these episodes, experience a feeling of humiliation. That experience is often followed by frustration, possibly anger, fear, guilt and then finally, depression. All these feelings eventually contribute to a worsening of the problem. The dysfunction creates these emotions and then they cyclically create further impotence. Often, it is a physical problem that is the primary cause of erection difficulties with the ensuing psychological factors experienced as a secondary response to the underlying physical problem.

The causes, as described in the previous chapter about how erections work, fall into three categories:

1. The inability to be able to initiate an erection.
2. The inability to fill the balloon-like chambers of the penis.
3. The inability to keep that blood in the penis for a sufficient length of time (after the balloon-like chambers have been filled), to achieve orgasm.

How Many Men Are Impotent?

At age 55, 8 per cent of all healthy men are impotent; at age 65, 25 per cent; at age 75, 55 per cent; and at age 80, as many as 75 per cent.

These figures reflect the fact that many men are impotent who don't need to be. Rather than looking at the 8 per cent who are impotent at 55, we might consider that 92 per cent are not; at age 65, 75 per cent are not; at age 75, 45 per cent are not and at age 80, 25 per cent are still performing.

Perhaps a change in life-style, a consultation with the doctor, and some much-needed education could solve the problem for many.

What Are The Major Common Causes Of Physical Impotence?

40%	Diabetes
30%	Vascular disease (such as arteriosclerosis)
13%	Radical pelvic surgery
8%	Spinal cord injury and pelvic fractures (often there is damage to the ability of the smooth-muscle tissue to relax. A complete

	severing of the spinal cord is more likely to cause total impotence than partial severing. Also, the location of the injury influences the degree of loss.
3%	Multiple sclerosis (plaques on the brain and the spinal cord interfere with the messages to the nerves).
1%	Other causes (including neurological disorders such as Parkinson's disease, Alzheimer's disease, uremia in kidney patients, endocrine disorders, alcoholism and certain medications).
95%	

The remaining 5% are psychological causes.

What Are The Major Common Causes Of Psychological Impotence?

- Religious beliefs
- Financial worries
- Business and/or career stress
- Relationship conflict
- Depression
- Premature ejaculation
- Vasectomy
- Mid-life crisis
- Lack of interest in sex

Why Is Diabetes Such A Major Cause Of Impotence?

Diabetes Mellitus is a disorder of carbohydrate metabolism and is the single leading cause of physical impotence.

There are two kinds of diabetes, Type I, or juvenile diabetes and Type II, adult-onset diabetes. Both types of diabetes tend to run in families. Sometimes the pancreas fails to generate sufficient insulin to handle the blood sugar levels adequately. In older people, it is more of a resistance to the action of insulin, rather than a lack of it.

Theoretically, if an individual lives long enough, anyone can become diabetic. In reality, approximately 1 out of 2 people is either diabetic or pre-diabetic. But heredity is not the only factor and diabetes is not passed from parent to child in an easily predictable way. A person's environment and lifestyle interact with heredity to determine whether a person will become diabetic.

Many people call this disease sugar diabetes and think that it is only the eating of sweets that causes it. In mature-onset diabetes, being overweight is the major risk factor. The exact role of obesity is unclear, but it is now considered that larger fat cells or larger numbers of fat cells demand more insulin than the body can produce (relative insulin deficiency) or the fat cells do not take up and utilise insulin properly (insulin resistance). Whatever the reason, being overweight and unexercised definitely contributes to Type II diabetes.

As people grow older, the diet may change and they may get less exercise, altering the glucose-insulin balance. Certain drugs can elevate blood sugar levels, including some of those used to treat high blood pressure.

Compared with the normal population, diabetics are 25 times more prone to blindness, 17 times more prone to kidney disease, five times more prone to gangrene, and twice as prone to heart disease. The nerves of diabetics can malfunction because of chemical abnormalities associated with high glucose levels or because of damage to the tiny supporting blood vessels. After age 40 the blood vessels that supply the limbs and the skin are affected.

Diabetes, which can go unobserved for a considerable length of time without any obvious symptoms, can eventually create damage to the small vessels and nerves in the penis. Both sensory and motor nerves can be affected. This damage can occur to the relaxation nerves to the penis and the endothelial cells that line the spaces in the erectile tissue. As these endothelial cells thin out, the valves which hold the blood in the erectile chambers no longer close completely and eventually they cease to function. Fifty per cent of all diabetics eventually become impotent. Certainly, this statistic alone, is sufficient reason for any man to attempt to control his weight and blood sugar levels.

Because the beginning of diabetes is without symptoms and in fact, the very first indication may be impotence, it is very important that diabetes be diagnosed and treated before it causes this nerve and tiny blood vessel damage.

What Hormones Might Be Involved In Impotence?

Sometimes impotence is hormonally related. It is estimated that hormonal imbalances may be responsible for as much as 35 per cent of impotence.

A number of hormones play a role in sexual functioning. Prolactin (a pituitary hormone) and thyroid (a hormone involved in growth, development and metabolism) may play a part in disturbances of sexual functioning.

Low testosterone (known as the male hormone) may contribute to impotence, but only in a secondary manner. There must be a drastic reduction in the amount of testosterone circulating in the blood before the mechanism of the erection is affected and castrated men are still able to perform sexually for as long as two years after castration.

While this hormone does not act directly on the penis, it is an important part of the sex drive. Without sufficient testosterone levels the male libido may be too low to generate enough interest in the sex act to maintain an erection adequate for intercourse.

There are numerous causes for inadequate hormones, including congenital abnormalities, genetic syndromes, drug therapies, exposure to toxins, radiation or difficulties with centres in the brain that regulate the production of hormones – the pituitary gland and the hypothalmus. Recently completed studies in the USA have indicated that a high-fat diet can contribute to low testosterone, which in turn can contribute to a low libido.

All these hormones can be tested with a simple blood test and if insufficient levels are pinpointed as the source of the problem, they can be treated easily and quickly with adequate hormonal replacement.

Is Impotence An Inevitable Consequence of Ageing?

A man is in his late teens to mid-20s is at his sexual peak. He produces the most sperm and requires the least time between erections.

University of Southern California researchers studied and compared men aged 19 to 30 with a similar number of men in the 48 to 65 age range; they had them all watch identical erotic films.

The younger men got erections almost six times faster. The circumference of the younger men's penises increased by an average of 1¼ inches, compared with not quite half an inch for the older men.

The average temperature of the younger men's penises rose by 4.3 degrees Fahrenheit (from a flaccid average temperature of 92.8), while that of the older men rose 2.1 degrees (from an already lower flaccid temperature of 91.7). Age lessened the physical sensitivity of the entire body, but after about age 65, the sensitivity of the penis declined greatly. These older men found pornographic films more exciting than tactile stimulation. This finding can be an important consideration for older men and it might be that changes in the way they deal with their sexuality will be necessary in order for them to become erect.

However, the study did not indicate that these older men were impotent. It simply showed they took longer to become aroused and that they preferred a different kind of stimulation from the younger men.

Many older men find it difficult to discuss the subject of impotence or difficulties with arousal with their doctor or friends. They often assume they will be the object of ridicule if they are concerned with being sexual at an age when many younger people think they should be beyond sexual desire.

Our culture is filled with jokes and subtle or not-so-subtle hints that older men and women should no longer concern themselves with sexual thoughts. Despite what the individual may feel, those messages are received and contribute to the inability of many older men to discuss impotence with anyone.

The fact is that healthy men, who are without major medically contributory factors, should be able to perform sexually well into their 80s and there are well-documented reports of men in their 90s who still function adequately.

In a study carried out by the National Institute on Aging in the USA, 2,622 adults over 60 were questioned about their sexuality. The results indicated that 91 per cent of men in their 60s were still having sex and 79 per cent after age 69. However, 90 per cent of the participants in this study rated their health as good to excellent.

Other investigations of less uniformly healthy older adult males paint a slightly different picture; sexual activity continued for half to two thirds of those in their 60s, with the fraction dropping to 25 per cent or less after age 75. For people in poor health or whose partner had died, it was easier for them to become celibate, rather than pursue a new partner or find a solution to the problem that was preventing them from being sexually active.

The Hunza, a group of people living in a high valley in India, are well known for their longevity and their virility. There are many factors which contribute to the long-term potency of the Hunza, including genetics, diet, activity, low stress, and life-style and cultural practices. There have been numerous attempts to emulate or adopt their life-style in other countries. These attempts have generally failed because their health and virility is more than just some magical life-style. It is the sum of everything that contributes to the well-being of the Hunza people.

However, the Hunzas do prove that a healthy and virile old age is possible, well beyond what other cultures have come to expect.

In various other cultures, many elderly couples are reporting that they continue to have enjoyable and satisfactory sexual relationships. So despite the cultural imperatives to 'get old' it is possible for healthy individuals to continue enjoying their sexual power.

Is There A Male Menopause?

Researchers at the St Louis University School of Medicine in the USA believe there is a male menopause. Scientists say that the production of the male hormone, testosterone, starts to decrease at about age 40 and drops sharply after age 60. They found that older men had less muscle strength, decreased libido, less energy and higher levels of cholesterol. The loss of this hormone contributed to frailty in some older men, but is not so obvious a marker as the loss of oestrogen for women, which usually precipitates profound alterations in body function such as the cessation of menstruation and loss of fertility. It appears that there are some men for whom there is a classical menopause with impotence, loss of desire, reduction in testicle size, reduction in beard and body hair growth and vague symptoms such as tiredness and hot flushes. Men with these symptoms were deemed hypogonadal and it is thought that about 10 per cent of older men fit the profile of a classic menopause.

It is possible that hormone replacement for better health and well-being might be appropriate for these men.

Do Older People Enjoy Sex As Much As Younger People?

In a large national study of older adults in the USA, 64 per cent of the men reported that the sex felt as good as or better than when they were younger. Several other investigations found that the interest and activity levels of earlier years strongly predicted one's sexual life after 60. Those who were indifferent to sex early on, found that the loss of an available partner or some other life-style change made it easy for them to just call it quits. Those who relished erotic activity during youth and mid-life, continued to pursue and desire a sexually exciting old age.

For sexually active older men, frequency declined with the passing years. Although there are wide variations in behaviour, someone who made love about twice a week during his early years dropped to twice a month after age 65.

Does Age Alter Physical Sexual Response?

Regardless of one's preferences, normal aging brings physical changes that alter sexual response.

As men grow older, they produce less testosterone, which correlates with lower sexual desire and activity. Genital sensitivity decreases also, because the peripheral nervous system loses sensory fibres and neurons. Generally, longer and more direct stimulation of the penis is needed to produce an erection.

The Japanese have invented an electron-scanning microscope able to view the most minute body structures. With this microscope it is possible to view the tiny veins that drain the erectile tissues. This microscope is able to give us a view of this tissue, showing that it becomes stiffer, less elastic and less able to expand as it ages. As it ages and hardens, it is less able to expand to press against the hard exterior coating of the penis, necessary to compress the venules against that coating, called the tunica, to close them off. These Japanese studies show that collagen, a fibrous protein material, becomes deposited in erectile tissue and causes this tissue to lose its ability to stretch and expand. These collagen deposits are associated with aging, diabetes and high cholesterol.

Sometimes, when these normal but potentially disturbing changes begin the couple abandon their sex life rather than consider how they might adapt - which may mean seeking outside advice and therapy or modifying how they make love.

Research indicates that in most cases the man stops initiating sexual relations and the woman just goes along with it. The couple go from no intercourse to no hugging, kissing or cuddling to not sleeping in the same bed to not sleeping in the same room. This premature end to sexual relationships could be avoided if couples knew more about normal sexual aging and were willing to be flexible.

In some ways, partners over 60 may have an unprecedented opportunity to become more biologically and emotionally synchronised. A older man's tendency to reach orgasm more slowly is well suited to the longer time a woman needs to become aroused. Birth control is no longer a problem, small children are not likely to interrupt at inopportune moments, and, if the couple have retired they have considerably more time to devote to being romantic.

When this type of collagen deposits occur in a young man, they are usually a result of scarring caused by injuries, sometimes from years earlier. It is possible to remove this scar tissue and restore potency in an operation called a crucal plication.

Are Impotent Men Sterile?

Impotence very rarely causes a man to be infertile and unable to achieve orgasm. It does not interfere with the ability to ejaculate and it does not damage sperm or interfere with the sex drive.

What Is Priapism?

Priapus, the son of Aphrodite and Dionysus, was a fertility god of ancient Greece and Rome, and he is usually represented with goat's horns, carrying a horn of plenty, holding a sickle in his hand and displaying a very large penis, rigid enough to support a basket of fruit. He was considered the protector of the vineyards and gardens, herds, bees and fish. The extremely large and erect penis of Priapus is only partly descriptive of the medical condition we now call priapism. Although Priapus was the god of fertility, the usual result of priapism is impotence and infertility.

Priapism is a painful, persistent and continuous erection, unaccompanied by sexual desire or excitement. At first thought, men might suppose this to be the ideal situation, but in actuality it becomes quite painful.

The mechanism for priapism is poorly understood, but it probably involves complex vascular and neurologic abnormalities. A clot in the pelvic area is most often thought to be the cause. This condition results from blood being trapped within the penis and upon examination is usually thick, dark blood, about the consistency of motor oil. The trapped blood then clots and forms scar tissue and once the scar tissue is in place the penis will no longer function in its normal manner and impotence occurs. If treated early with clot dissolving medications, ice enemas, and drugs to lower high blood pressure, the impotence can be reversed, but once the scar tissue occurs, the resulting impotence can only be treated with prosthetic implants.

About 40 per cent of the men who suffer from priapism also have sickle cell anaemia, a disorder which distorts the blood cell into a crescent shape, making passage through the veins difficult.

What Is Peyronie's Disease?

No cause is known, no virus, bacteria or chemical has been identified as the source of the condition. The only statistical association of any significance is with moderate alcohol intake and that similar scarring process in the hand called 'Dupuytren's contracture', in which the tendons allowing the ring and little fingers to close into a fist are pulled by scar tissue into a permanently clenched position.

Peyronie's disease results in scar tissue forming on the walls of the lining that covers the chambers of the penis that normally fill with blood during an erection. When this scar formation occurs, the penis begins to curve to one side, since the scar tissue is hard and unelastic. This scarring can also decrease the blood flow within the penis, sometimes resulting in painful erections; if the curvature becomes severe enough, it becomes impossible to have intercourse. When this happens, the scar tissue is surgically removed and replaced with a graft of the inner skin layer, the dermis, obtained from the thigh or lower abdomen. These grafts are not always successful when the condition is advanced. If this is the case, then the solution is often a penile implant, a prosthesis.

Can High Cholesterol Cause Impotence?

In order to have an erection, a man must fill the two balloon-like chambers of the penis with blood; to sustain that erection, 20 times the normal amount of blood must circulate through the penis. One of the problems with high cholesterol is that blood vessels carrying blood to the various organs of the body can get partially or completely blocked with cholesterol, and the penis is just one of those organs. Or a man may be able to become erect, only to find that after intercourse has begun, he is unable to sustain the erection. Because of clogged arteries, the buttock muscles, which require additional blood at this time, remove blood from the penis, which is already receiving a reduced blood flow, to supply those muscles.

A recent study found that the levels of testosterone fell by 30 per cent in men within four hours of eating a meal containing 57 per cent fat. These hormone levels stayed the same when the meal contained only 2 per cent fat.

Interestingly, despite a continuous flood of information in the media about cholesterol's relationship to heart disease and heart attack deaths, there is almost no mention of its involvement in impotence.

The risk of death from heart attack by the average man with normal cholesterol levels is 50 per cent. Those same risk factors for heart disease are risk factors for impotence. Lower your cholesterol and you lower your heart attack risk, at the same time lowering your impotency risk.

The bad cholesterol number is changing all the time. The current thought is that your cholesterol should be no more than your age plus 100. If it is higher than that, you are at risk for impotence.

What Is The 'Steal Syndrome'?

When there are problems with the blood supply to the penis from arterial insufficiency and the man begins to expend energy in sexual intercourse, he finds himself having to deal with the 'steal syndrome'. The large muscles of the buttocks and thighs require additional blood and oxygen for the act of thrusting and will divert blood from the erection in order to fuel these muscles. The man may begin intercourse with a fairly firm erection only to find that he loses it shortly thereafter.

Can Problems With Penile Arteries Be The Cause Of Impotence?

Arteries bring fresh, oxygenated blood to the body part requiring it. There are erection arteries that run through each of the balloon-like structures of the penis. Since arteries are thick, muscular vessels, they can constrict and maintain the high pressure required to maintain an erection. If these arteries are diseased, such as when plaque deposits line them, or if they have become rigid and unelastic, they are likely to be unable to provide sufficient blood to the penis to inflate the two erectile chambers.

Can Problems With Veinous Valves Be The Cause Of Impotence?

The veins have small valves in them which prevent the blood flow from returning to the heart and emptying the penis of blood after ejaculation. Unfortunately, these valves can become leaky with age. In younger men problems with the veins are more likely to be caused by a congenital abnormality of the vessels or the result of an injury.

Can Stress Cause Impotence?

Stress is quite difficult to define. What one person finds stressful may mean nothing to the next, but anything which influences the libido may affect potency. For one man that might be being overworked, a family argument, loss of status for whatever reason; all these things can be considered stress and that stress can affect the libido which can then result in loss of potency. This is one of the reasons why many men have been told "it's all in your head" and why a medical examination is the best way to uncovering the true cause of the problem.

When a man is unable to get an erection, his body responds to that stress by pumping adrenaline through his body. This has the effect of draining the blood from the penis and halts any beginning erection.

In a study comparing men's worst fears with those of women, it was found that men's top five fears were:

1. Being physically inadequate. Men don't want to appear weak or unmasculine. Being strong and competing successfully is very important to men.
2. Showing emotion. Men were good at expressing anger but showing other emotions like caring and love was frightening to them.
3. Powerful women. Men felt threatened by female bosses and didn't like it if their wives earned more money than them. They needed to be in control both at work and at home.
4. Being intellectually inferior. Men didn't want to appear unknowledgeable, even if they weren't. They worried about feeling less smart or ambitious than fellow workers.
5. Failure. Men were very afraid of getting fired or being told that they were incompetent. This fear of failure included the dread of being impotent, of not being a great lover.

When any of these fears became real or even just a worry, they had a great impact on the ability to have an erection.

In contrast, women's top five fears were:

1. Being cut off from loved ones.
2. Being unattractive.
3. Being a victim of violence.
4. Displeasing others.
5. Failing at relationships.

None of the fears of women related to the inability to perform sexually – a fear that is unique to men and can be part of their stress syndrome.

Can Having A Heart Attack Cause Impotence?

Sometimes after recovery from a heart attack a man may find that he is impotent. While the heart attack itself did not cause this to happen, the frightening concern that the extra exertion of intercourse may cause another heart attack can lead to impotence. As many as 25 per cent of men who have a major heart attack never again resume sex and 50 per cent who do resume it, do so at a reduced frequency.

In most cases, anyone who can tolerate an exercise stress test that raises the heart rate to 120 beats per minute can safely engage in sexual intercourse. In fact, some studies indicate that an active sex life is beneficial for people with heart disease because of its exercise value. Nevertheless, some people take a nitroglycerin tablet shortly before making love as a precaution against chest pain.

The fear of suffering a second heart attack may be a needless worry. Some statistics show that fewer than one per cent of sudden coronary deaths occur during intercourse and seven out of ten of these have occurred during extramarital sex. This has lead researchers to believe that the stress of the guilt that accompanies extramarital sex, as well as the fear of being discovered, may contribute to the coronary accident, rather than the actual physical exertion of the sex act itself.

Does A Vasectomy Cause Impotence?

Vasectomy, the male sterilisation procedure, is a method used for permanent contraception. Men who have had a vasectomy have continued ability to have intercourse and normal erections. In addition, they notice almost little or no change in the physical appearance of their semen, because the semen contains such a small amount of sperm in the fluids.

The severing of the vasa deferentia, known as a vasectomy, only prevents the conduction of the sperm from the testes to the urethra. Any impotence that occurs is probably associated with the thinking that no longer being able to father children is unmanly.

What Effect Can Fetishes Have On Potency?

There are men who require their sexual partner to be dressed in a particular way, require a particular object to be held or certain words to be said in order to be potent. If this is the case, this can be considered evidence of fetishism, the worship of an inanimate object as a symbol of a loved person.

The subconscious plays a large part in the selection of fetishes and these associations can go back to forgotten childhood memories. It is fairly easy when the fetish object is a commonplace object such as a shoe (one of the more common fetish objects). However, sometimes these fetishes and the rituals that accompany them can become very complicated or difficult to obtain.

Unfortunately, some men may become selectively impotent when deprived of their fetish object.

If this should occur, it is probably best to work with a therapist who specialises in sexual problems in order to remove the need for a fetish or perhaps replace it with something more obtainable.

Can Penile Nerves Be The Source Of Impotence?

Two types of nerves are involved in the erection process. First there are those nerves which record the touch in the skin of the penis, particularly the glans, the highly sensitive head of the penis. These nerves are called the *peripheral sensory nerves*. Then there are those nerves which tell the smooth-muscle tissue of the spaces in the penis to relax, allowing the penis to fill with blood and causing the system to close off and keep that blood within the penis. These nerves are called the motor autonomic nerves.

Since an erection is completely dependent on electrical signals from the brain to the penis, causing it to expand and retain the blood, these electrical circuits can have any number of malfunctions. Pressure from a prolapsed spinal disc; a deteriorated disc, which puts pressure on the nerve; particular nerve diseases, such as multiple sclerosis or diabetes, which damage the nerves; strokes, tumours or a sports injury to the groin or pelvic area, often those injuries called a straddle injury, such as can be caused by the pressure of a bicycle seat. All these things can cause this electrical system to malfunction.

When the impotence is neurologically-based, it is quite often associated with other symptoms. There may be difficulty in controlling the bowel or bladder. There may be a loss of sensation in the general genital area. The anal sphincter may be lax. And the reflex called the bulbocavernosus reflex – which causes the anal sphincter to contract when the head of the penis is squeezed – is likely to be lost.

Why Does A Man Have A Morning Erection Without Sexual Thoughts?

When the penis is flaccid, very little blood passes through to the spongy tissue that makes up the erectile tissue. At the time of erection, the tiny valves which act like trap doors close off and the penis becomes filled with blood. These same tiny valves block the outflow of blood so that the penis remains filled. When the erection leaves, this process is reversed and the shunt outflow valves open. These valves are activated in two ways. Sexual or amorous thoughts send messages to these valves through the sympathetic nerves, or direct stimulation of the penis activates them through a reflex, the involuntary nervous system. This kind of reflex is similar to the knee jerk reaction when the knee is struck by the doctor with a small instrument to see if the leg will then move.

A morning erection is a similar reflex reaction, through the spinal column and the involuntary nervous system. This reflex responds to the stimulation of a full bladder. This reflexive erection is a good indication that the nervous system connections, circulation and hormone levels are normal and in good operating condition.

What Effect Does Smoking Have On Potency?

Nicotine is a well-known vasoconstrictor. One of the effects of this drug is to make all the body's blood vessels contract. Any time a blood vessel contracts less blood will be able to enter or leave the arteries and veins. These contractions ultimately damage the very tiny blood vessels, known as capillaries, which form a network between the arterioles and the venules, the larger structures of the circulatory system, in all parts of the body. Since the penis is entirely dependent upon blood flow to fill the corpora cavernosa, it is readily apparent that smoking, in any amount, should affect the erectile tissue of the penis. Several researchers found that some patients who stopped smoking were able to regain sexual function.

What Effect Does Alcohol Have On Potency?

Alcohol is a vasodilator, a drug that enlarges the blood vessels, allowing for a greater blood flow and often causing the individual to feel warm. However, as the blood vessels near the surface of the body are expanded, they are subject to the outside temperatures which are usually much lower than normal body temperature and the blood close to the surface is cooled, causing the vessels to contract again. This can become complicated as the vessels expand and contract in relation to the effects of the alcohol and the attempts of the body to bring the blood to the surface and then return it to the heart.

In addition, new research indicates that alcohol also decreases the body's ability to produce testosterone, creating in effect, a male menopause, decreasing the libido or sex drive and affecting sexual function. There is an enzyme of testosterone known as dihydroxytestosterone, which is broken down by another bodily enzyme whose job it is to break down alcohol. When this enzyme goes to work on the alcohol, it also breaks down the testosterone enzyme, dihydroxytestosterone, resulting in lower testosterone levels. At the same time this enzyme also stimulates the production of a hormone which causes an increase in femininising characteristics, such as enlarged breasts and shrunken testicles.

Unfortunately, while alcohol in small amounts reduces anxiety, lowers inhibitions and frees up sexual response, in anything over a small amount, it has just the opposite effect: it acts as an anaesthetic, desensitises the penis and reduces sexual response.

William Masters and Virginia Johnson, the famed sex researchers, revolutionised the way sex is researched and their published results were very different from previous thinking. They found, in their laboratory studies, that most men experience their first failed erection while under the influence of alcohol. Studies of chronic alcoholics indicate that 80 per cent of them have radically decreased sex drives or are impotent.

Can Medication Cause Impotence?

There is a long list of medications that cause impotence. Some of the most notorious are those given for high blood pressure, ulcers and epilepsy. Often, the physician, in the interests of the overall health of the patient, may even neglect to inform the patient of the potential for impotence, because he knows that the patient will probably stop taking the medication.

Should you suspect that your medication may be the culprit, it is best to discuss it with your doctor. There may be other medications that work just as well for your condition.

Can Recreational Drugs Cause Impotence?

Cocaine, opiates, heroin, marijuana, morphine, amphetamines and barbiturates all affect the ability to function sexually. Several of them block serotonin in the brain and increase the levels of dopamine. Cannabis initially makes sex better, causing the users to relax whilst increasing their sense of touch. 60 per cent of the male users said it increased the intensity of orgasm. Marijuana directly affects the metabolism of testosterone and eventually affects the libido. Cocaine has been called the champagne of sex drugs because it not only affects desire but increases sensitivity of the penis. Angel dust, mescaline and LSD are reported to amplify the feelings of touch also.

However, ultimately, their effects are either to decrease the sex drive or adversely affect the nervous system. An imbalance in dopamine and serotonin can eventually have very adverse effects on the functioning of the nervous system and requires cessation of all recreational chemicals to be returned to normal functioning.

Can Exercise Cause Impotence?

When a person exercises excessively, it stimulates the body's naturally-occurring opiates, the endorphins. We have all heard of 'runner's high', a phenomenon believed to occur because the extreme of this exercise causes the body to release endorphins that keep the runner from feeling the pain.

The amount of exercise necessary to keep in good shape is beneficial and fun but beyond a certain point the body protects itself from the pain by releasing endorphins. These same endorphins can prevent men from feeling the stimulation of sexual contact, resulting in a period of impotence.

Do Steroids Cause Impotence?

Body builders believe that anabolic steroids – primarily the male sex hormone, testosterone – build up muscle tissue and strength. Steroids are powerful chemicals that the body manufactures to control sexual development, metabolism and other functions.

In adults, adverse reactions occur with the use of anabolic steroids, including testicular atrophy and impotence. Anabolic steroids reduce the number of disease-fighting white cells in the blood and increase concentrations of cholesterol, known to affect the lining of the blood vessels and contribute to reduced blood flow, which affects erection.

Does Pain Cause Impotence?

When a man is in extreme pain, sexual intercourse is far from his mind. However, when in pain, the body produces its own opiates, the endorphins. These naturally-occurring opiates can turn off any sexual stimuli.

Can Just The Fear Of 'Another Failure' Cause Impotence?

A man can trigger the sympathetic nervous system just by being too anxious: one episode of impotence may be enough to trigger the sympathetic nervous system the next time he approaches intercourse. For some men, the fear of failure is so overwhelming that it floods the body with norepinephrine, an adrenal hormone, creating the opposite physical environment to the one necessary to have an erection.

Does Having An Unusually Large Penis Contribute To Impotence?

It has been thought, based on the need to fill the erectile chambers with blood, that a larger penis required more blood and therefore would be more likely to suffer from a failed blood supply and resulting impotence However, it appears that a man's vascular system is engineered to provide the proper blood supply for his particular needs and penis size presents no additional problem.

Can Prostate Surgery Cause Impotence?

Radical pelvic surgery for prostate cancer or colon cancer may lead to impotence; however, recent potency-sparing prostate operations for prostatic cancer appear to help preserve potency. New laser surgeries and the implanting of radio-active seeds into the prostate gland not only increase the survival rates, but greatly reduce the trauma of the erectile structures.

Routine transurethral prostatectomy for obstruction has a very low incidence of impotence - approximately 6 to 8 per cent.

Can Individuals With Spinal Cord Injuries And Paralysis Have Erections?

Erections are under the control of a set of nerves that receive messages from the brain through the electrical circuits of the spinal cord. The higher up in the spinal cord the injury occurs, the more likely it is that the man will be able to have an erection.

A surprising 80 to 90 per cent of men with extensive paralysis are able to achieve erections. It would appear that there is a set of primitive reflexes that can be stimulated by trigger points on the inner thighs or under the testicles, bypassing the electrical circuitry of the nervous system. Because of the additional psychological effect of arousal, many of these patients will be able to maintain sufficient erection for intercourse and orgasm.

Does Dialysis Cause Impotence?

Sometimes abnormal hormones are produced during the process of dialysis and this can lead to impotence. Current research is underway to develop new machines which will decrease the incidence of impotence associated with the process of dialysis.

What Is Primary Impotence?

Some men have never been potent and this may be due to vascular or neurological causes, often because of a birth defect. A person who has never had an erection should have a medical evaluation to discover the cause.

Why Are Some Men Only Able To Be Potent When They Masturbate?

A man who is impotent only at a time of sexual interactions with others but not with masturbation usually has a type of impotence that is psychogenic or psychological in nature. This type of impotence can usually be treated successfully with psychological therapy.

3 Facts, Myths and Fantasies

Ancient man thought that the penis was a living entity separate from the body of the human to which it was attached. They thought it was a divinity which had been sent to them from the heavens.

Over the centuries, myths, magic and fantasies have been associated with the penis, its ability to become erect and the things that might affect that ability.

The penis has figured in law, in magic and in mythology. Man has spent innumerable hours and money in an attempt to control the life and ways of this erratic part of their anatomy. In all languages, whether primitive or developed, the penis has been described as being an individual. Sometimes it is given a separate and individual name, usually a masculine name and in any conversation the penis is nearly always referred to as 'he' rather than 'it'.

Historically, Man has always wished for an absolutely foolproof concoction that would ensure that the sexual partner of his dreams would be so driven with lust for him that she would want and dream only of him. He also wanted something that would turn him into a super-stud, so virile that he would be able to perform endlessly.

From the beginning of human history right up to the present, alchemists and scientists have brewed up love potions. The gods and goddesses of mythology, the sorcerers of ancient times, the witch doctors, the voodoo priests and priestesses, the purveyors of strange bottles of mysterious elixirs which were sold from the back of horse-drawn wagons by the travelling medicine men, quacks and herbalists, scientists and pharmacists; all have pursued the dream of finding that wonderful potion that would make these fantasies a reality. Most of the potions were connected to magic and were bought by individuals based on the hope of wish fulfilment rather than anything based on reality.

There have been quite a few famous lovers during the course of history and men of great wealth, social prominence, fame or professional superiority are often able to attract droves of admirers and lovers. Even obviously ugly or notoriously ill-tempered men, if they have fame or wealth, have been able to attract almost any woman they chose. It has been said of these men that power, raw power, indeed, may be the ultimate aphrodisiac.

What follows are some of the facts, myths and fantasies thought to affect the penis. While many are fascinating, none seem to have any real validity. Still, they reflect the thinking and yearnings of other cultures and other times, about the causes and treatment of impotence and the lengths to which men will go to remain or become potent.

Why Were Young Boys Told That Masturbation Would Cause Blindness, Brain Damage And Impotence?

Many parents, in the hope of stopping their children from masturbating and delay telling them about the facts of life, told terrifying tales of the evils of sex and the effects of masturbation.

Some of these tales have their foundations in ideas from ancient times concerning the content of the seminal fluids. Albert Camus, the French author and journalist, whose writings profoundly influenced the conscience of Western thought and who was considered one of the great thinkers of his time, wrote that the fluid of ejaculate contained microscopic amounts of brain matter. Camus apparently got his belief from Hippocrates, the Greek physician who lived in 460 B.C. and was called the father of medicine. Hippocrates compiled some highly speculative theories on physiology and disease, including the theory that the loss of semen caused a disease responsible for the wasting away of the spine. Some five hundred years later, his theory was further promulgated by Aulus Celsus, the 1st century A.D. Roman encyclopaedist, whose writings included not only the most complete Roman medical text of his time, but also a history of early medicine.

Celsus's *De Medicina* drew largely on earlier Greek medical writers and covered the whole of medicine including surgery, nutrition, pharmacology, hygiene and mental disease. Because Celsus was an encyclopaedist, not a physician, he often accepted the opinions of Hippocrates, perpetuating the erroneous thinking about the deleterious effects of the loss of seminal fluid.

The yogis of ancient India practised stilling the breath to control the Kundulini, a coiled serpent that was thought to reside at the base of the spine, believing that random sexual thoughts would interfere with it. It was thought that the loss of semen, whether through masturbation or sexual intercourse, caused this serpent to rise up through the spinal cord, keeping the yogi from attaining Nirvana, a higher level of development. The loss of semen would prevent any man from attaining that much desired enlightenment that the yogi strived for his entire life.

In 17th century America masturbation was illegal and when young boys masturbated in a group and then one of them talked about the experience, the crime would be discovered. The penalty was a public whipping with a heavy leather strap, often severe enough to cause bleeding and other injuries as well as shame and embarrassment.

In the 1800s leading European doctors suggested that excessive masturbation caused the body to become debilitated, as it was thought that the body's vital forces would drain out with the semen, causing tuberculosis, epilepsy and insanity. Other doctors wrote that untreated chronic loss of semen caused weakness of the mind, dullness and an irregular heartbeat. These doctors suggested that you could readily detect a regular masturbator because of his pale complexion, watery eyes, shrunken sex organs and poor memory.

The Victorian era, with its negative attitude towards sexuality and prim religious beliefs, recommended that children be put to bed with their hands tied to the bedpost.

In the early 1800s it was even recommended that an egg-shaped object be inserted into the rectum to press on the prostate gland. The concept was that this would force the ejaculate into the bladder and conserve the 'vital life force'.

These eggs can still be seen in antique shops, made of wood, metal and decorated porcelain.

A variety of drugs were prescribed to avoid excessive loss of semen, including quinine, digitalis and opium, so fearful was the thought of the loss of the 'vital fluid'. Parents were willing to do anything to keep their young sons from becoming seriously ill from the effects of this sinful masturbation and thus avoid their premature deaths.

With the advent of more sophisticated medical thinking, the belief that loss of seminal fluid was harmful disappeared, but there is still an echo of these beliefs to be found in those who wish to control the masturbatory habits and blossoming sexuality of young adolescents.

Where Does The Word 'Testify' Come From?

In Biblical times, an oath was taken by placing of a man's hand on his own testicles, or on the testicles of another, when making a pledge, whether it was of allegiance or some other kind of serious and solemn promise. It was believed that in doing so a man was indicating his responsibility to the yet unborn offspring of both himself and the individual to whom he swore his sacred vow. It also reminded the testifier that these unborn generations, who would carry the bloodlines of both, would have the right and obligation to revenge, should the vow fail to be kept.

In Roman times, the eunuch, or the castrated man, could not testify in court; there are many Biblical references to swearing on or testifying by 'the stones' (testicles).

Why Were Eunuchs In Charge Of Harems?

The sultans and kings of ancient times had many wives and harems and wanted someone they believed they could trust to keep an eye on them. The word eunuch, which comes from the Greek, means 'keeper of the bed'.

It is thought that the Persians were the first to castrate men specifically for this purpose and the practice then spread to other parts of the world. Often, because of their reputation for trustworthiness and organisational abilities, the eunuchs became military commanders, administrators and advisers to those kings or princes they served.

Castration usually took place before puberty. Prisoners of war were often castrated with the idea that they would become more placid and manageable. Eunuchs who were to become keepers of the harem would have both the testicles and the penis removed.

When castration was done before puberty eunuchs became tall and thin because the male hormone, which ends the growth of the long bones of the arms and legs, did not circulate. If castrated after puberty, which was often the case with the prisoners, they would become fat.

Because the male hormone testosterone is responsible for the production of secondary sex characteristics, eunuchs did not become bald. Depending on the age at which the castration took place, their hair pattern stayed at whatever stage it was then.

Who Were The Castrati?

During the 16th century, prepubescent boys with particularly fine singing voices were castrated so that they might continue to sing with beautifully clear and soprano or alto voices for the glory of God. Their beautiful voices, the result of castration in childhood, produced a powerful, unique sound of great range. The combination of the larynx of a youth and the chest and lungs of a fully grown man gave the voice an unparalled resonance. These heavenly choirs of castrated males were known as Castrati. They were particularly popular in the churches and opera in Europe during the 17th and 18th centuries. These most famous choirs were greatly admired and great composers wrote special music for their angelic voices. In the 18th century the Pope decreed the practice should be discontinued and it was left to literature to describe the extraordinary beauty of the sound of these great choirs, based on the suffering and the sacrifice of so many young boys.

Can Your Penis Size Be Determined By The Size Of Your Fingers?

There are stories that the size of a man's penis can be determined by looking at his hands, nose, feet or ears.

The size of the penis varies from man to man; it is impossible to judge its size from any of these other organs. Researchers at the Masters and Johnson Institute in the USA say that they are no longer interested in penis size.

They think that it has almost no significance in their serious research and they feel that it is the kind of information that just makes most people uncomfortable.

Other researchers indicate that the average length of the erect adult male penis is approximately 6 inches and approximately 4.4 inches in circumference. When the penis is flaccid there is considerable variation and size can be influenced by both temperature and stress.

How Large Is The Average Penis?

There are a variety of studies with differing results. An 1899 study showed that the average relaxed penis was about 3.7 inches, with the range extending from 2.9 to 4.5 inches. Average flaccid circumference was 3.5 inches.

A 1949 study, which averaged the results of nine different studies, placed the average flaccid length at 3.9 inches, with a range of 2.4 to 4.5 inches. The average erect length was 6.1 inches, with a range of 4.7 to 8.3 inches. In this study, the average flaccid circumference was 3.3 inches with a range of 3 to 4.1 inches and the average erect circumference was 4.3 inches with a range of 3.3 to 4.7 inches.

Alfred Kinsey's research, which was limited to 1,500 adult white males, placed the average erect length at 6.2 inches with 90 per cent of the organs measuring in the 5 to 7.5 inch range.

When Masters and Johnson were still willing to discuss size, they found the normal penis measured between 3.4 and 4.1 inches when flaccid. They found, however, that relaxed size was not a reliable indication of erect size. They compared the erections of one group whose relaxed organs measured between 3 and 3.5 inches with a second group whose organs measured between 3.9 and 4.5 inches and found that smaller organs increased in size more than larger ones. The smaller ones showed increases of between 6 to 6.7 inches, while the increase shown by larger organs ranged between 2.8 and 3 inches for totals between 6.7 to 7.5 inches.

Still another group of researchers found that the average Caucasian male's penis is between 3 and 4 inches long when flaccid, averaging 3.7 inches, with a circumference of 2.5 to 4 inches.

Normally, an erection adds about 50 to 60 per cent to the penis length. When this percentage is added upon erection the average male will have an erect penis of approximately 6 inches – varying between 4.7 and 7 inches – with a circumference of 3.2 to 4.7 inches.

Dr Kinsey found that about 24 per cent of men have a penis which is within the average range. Approximately 5 per cent have an erect penis of less than 3.5 inches and only 1 in 100 has an erect penis longer than 9 inches and 1 in 10,000 measures 10 inches in length.

The alleged racial and ethnic differences in penis size have not been addressed in serious studies and physicians who deal with the male sex organ in the course of their medical practices have said that such differences do not exist.

However, other researchers disagree, saying that there are racial differences, with people of colour from Africa having an average penis length of 5 to 5.75 inches when flaccid and 7.5 to 8 inches when erect. Asiatic men's penises average 5 inches erect, while the Eastern Indian's penis length averages 4 to 4.5 inches in the erect state.

Is Penis Size Important To Women?

When Shere Hite, the sex researcher, interviewed women about sex, they rarely mentioned penis size as an important factor in their choice of sex partner. In a similar survey, another researcher questioned almost 500 women; and there was not a single mention of the importance of penis size.

There is agreement among sex researchers that the size of a man's penis has very little to do with the ability to please a women sexually. The touch-sensitive nerve endings of the vagina lie almost exclusively in the organ's forwardmost third, a distance of approximately two inches. The interior can feel only pressure and thus receives only minor additional stimulation. The cervix, at the very back of the vagina has few nerve endings; minor surgery can be performed on the cervix without anaesthesia. Penile circumference does not appear to play a significant physical role in female satisfaction. The normal vagina is capable of alternately and snugly accommodating a pencil, a baby's head or a penis of virtually any circumference.

In addition, at some point during intercourse, the deep walls of the vagina expand away from the penis to create a basin for the reception of semen. This basin is created in order to hold the semen close to the cervical opening and allow the optimum opportunity for impregnation. At this time the penis is barely in contact with the deeper walls of the vagina, something most women are completely unaware of.

Is Penis Size Important To Men?

According to sex researcher Alex Comfort, penis size sits near the top of the list of sexual concerns of the male.

When men express concern about penis size, they usually refer to length, not girth. Men are accustomed to equating size with power and strength and the locker-room comparisons are games young boys play with each other in their long road to manhood. This thinking is reinforced by sexual publications and the X-rated movie industry and may contribute to unnecessary insecurities in young boys.

How Is Penis Length Measured?

This information is of interest only when measuring for the proper fitting of a penile implant and will be done correctly by the urologist.

The correct way to measure the penis is from the top, with the measuring instrument pressed snugly against the pubic bone. Measuring underneath, while it will give a larger number, is not correct.

What Determines Penis Size?

All foetuses are female from the time of conception until other genetic factors take over. The sex of the child is determined by the father's genes. The male hormone testosterone is the major contributor to the size of the male penis. In the first 12 to 14 weeks of life, the amount of testosterone the male will produce is determined by the hormone production of the mother, which is in turn determined by her genetic background. After the fourteenth week the male foetus begins to produce its own hormones and if the level of testosterone is insufficient, the penis will not develop. When this happens, the resultant child will be a hermaphrodite, in which both male and female organs are present.

Beginning at about ten weeks after conception, the penis will grow at the rate of .03 inch a week to approximately 1.5 inches at birth.

How Does The Penis Develop?

Until about the 35th day after fertilisation, the gonads of the foetus are indistinguishable as to sex. Soon after the 35th day the male foetus begins producing testosterone and its presence stimulates the development of the male genitalia. Without testosterone, female genitalia will develop. Three tiny elements on the underside of the foetus – the genital tubercle, the genital folds and the genital swellings – begin to change.

The tubercle, the closest of the three to the navel, forms the glans, or head of the penis. In the female, it forms the glans or head of the clitoris.

The two genital folds, situated behind and to either side of the tubercle, grow toward one another and fuse at the midline. The tube thus formed is the shaft of the penis; it lines up precisely with the developing glans. In the female, these folds do not join, but grow to form the inner labia of the vagina. Meanwhile, the genital swellings, which are the farthest to the rear, begin fusing in like-manner to form the scrotum. In the female, this becomes the vagina's outer labia.

This process is essentially complete 12 weeks after fertilisation, when the sitting height of the foetus is about 3.5 inches and the newly-formed penis is about a quarter of an inch long.

Does The Penis Have A Bone?

The penis of the human male has no bone, although the penises of most other mammals have a bone that keeps the penis of these mammals in a constant state of semi-erection.

Are Monkey Glands And Injections Of Sheep Hormones Of Any Value In Maintaining Youth And Potency?

Clinics throughout Europe advertise injections made from the cells of sheep, for both virility and to reverse the aging process. These clinics cater to the very wealthy and famous. Several well-known movie actors, as well as other celebrities, have endorsed such procedures. There is no documented scientific evidence that these sheep cells do anything, outside of the placebo effect they may have and the rest and pampering one gets at such clinics.

In the early 1900s, experiments were undertaken in an attempt to graft the testicles of healthy young male monkeys into aging, impotent men. These experiments were a failure. Unfortunately, rumours exist that such surgeries work. They do not.

What Is The Purpose Of The Foreskin?

The head of the penis is covered with a dense network of nerve endings and is more sensitive to touch than any other part of the body; it is the purpose of the foreskin to protect this sensitive tip. The foreskin is equipped with specialised glands that squeeze out an oily substance on the penile head to prevent it from drying out and to protect it from the environment, bacteria and fungus.

Why Did Circumcision Become So Universal?

In modern times circumcision has generally been regarded as a prophylactic against some diseases; in antiquity it was also considered a substitute for human sacrifice to the gods, an offering of part of the cherished human body. This allowed male children to live and still was thought to satisfy the gods. From prehistoric myth to religious practice, circumcision has become almost universally practiced.

Some Biblical scholars speculate that the mark of Cain, as described in the Bible, was actually a mark of circumcision. Most anthropologists agree that circumcision is associated with the preparation for and initiation into, the age of virility. It may have had its origins in ancient Egypt and there appears to be proof that the Canaanites, who appeared in western Asia as early as 3 B.C., were the first to include it as part of their religious ceremonies. It is part of the transition from boyhood to manhood in Polynesia, Australia and throughout Africa.

Because the foreskin excretes an oily lubricating substance, known as smegma (the cheesy substance that collects under the foreskin of the uncircumcised male), that was thought to be a breeding ground for disease. And indeed, in believing this, primitive peoples were being practical and accurate, because this smegma can be a source of bacterial and fungal infections if not frequently removed. In some desert cultures, where water was scarce and driving sand could collect under the foreskin, it was a practical consideration.

It is further thought that the origins of the practice of circumcision were for reasons of hygiene and that those logical hygienic reasons became entangled with myth and then religion. The obvious hygienic reasons for circumcision evolved into both religions, as a covenant with God and ceremony, as a rite of passage for pubescent boys.

Today, with the exception of religious beliefs and practices, there does not seem to be any sound reason for circumcision and a young male child can be taught to retract his foreskin and cleanse the glans of his penis at bath time, just as he is taught other hygienic practices.

What Is The Sex Flush?

During intercourse, blood pools in certain organs. The belly area decreases in temperature; the skin over the chest increases in temperature. The entire penis increases in temperature as much as two degrees higher than the overall body temperature. This cooling of the skin in some areas and warming in the sex organs reflects a divergence of blood from one area to the other.

Vasocongestion occurs in both the penis of the male and the clitoris of the female. The breasts of both sexes increase in size by about 20 per cent. This localised blood pooling includes a flush covering the chest and breasts and is caused by the dilation of small blood vessels in the skin. This flush disappears almost immediately after orgasm.

What Happens At Ejaculation?

When a man has an orgasm there is a rapid, recurring, involuntary but highly coordinated contraction of several muscles in the groin, as well as of the urethra. The contractions start at intervals of an eighth of a second and decrease rapidly after the first three or four.

Most men expel between 0.06 and 0.17 of an ounce of fluid. In 85 per cent of men, all the sperm in one ejaculation (between 120 and 200 million) are expelled in the first spurt with enough force to send them approximately two feet – sufficient to fertilise any available ovum.

What Does 'Feeling Your Oats' Mean?

In English folklore, both the expressions, 'feeling your oats' or 'sowing wild oats' are meant to express frisky and lusty behaviour or rampant promiscuity in the exuberance of youth. Possible origins of these expressions may refer to the fact that a horse well-fed is energetic and may prance; as well as to the knowledge that the seed of wild grasses will take root in almost any soil when scattered by the wind.

Recent scientific studies have shown that oats decrease the cholesterol levels in the blood, increasing the blood's ability to circulate. Oats have also been shown to increase the levels of the biologically active male hormone testosterone in the bloodstream. It may be that these expressions reflected the awareness of the increased vitality that came from regularly eating a healthy food.

What Is Spanish Fly?

Spanish Fly is the most famous of the so-called aphrodisiacs. This powder is made by grinding the dried bodies of a beetle called cantharis. One spoonful of Spanish Fly added to food causes a stinging and burning sensation in the vagina or of the penis, caused by the pooling of blood in the pelvis. The result is either an erection or an itching of the sexual organs, which make them intensely sensitive. This results in the need to rub the pubic area.

Who Was Saint Vinegar?

Priapus, the Greek god of crops and herds and the son of Aphrodite and Dionysus, was the god of sexuality. With the advent of Christianity, Priapus took on the persona of different saints and large phalli were carved out of wooden logs to represent him. Barren women who prayed to become fertile would scrape wood off these penis-like logs and mix the sawdust with water and wine. They would drink the mixture themselves or administer it to their lovers, in the hope that it would bring sexual potency and result in pregnancy. At Priapus festivals, women would pour wine over these phalli-saints and then collect and drink the wine after it had soured. This drink, thought to have magical powers of fertility and potency, was referred to by the French as 'Saint Vinegar'.

Why Does Sunlight Enhance The Sex Drive?

Sunlight has been found to stimulate the pituitary gland, which regulates the testicles.

The lack of daylight is a signal for the brain's pineal gland to produce melatonin, a substance that inhibits sperm production and the hormones that are responsible for sexual desire.

The lowest levels of testosterone occur around 11 o'clock at night and the highest just at sunrise.

Men's highest levels of testosterone during the year occur in the months of optimum sunlight, in the summer and early autumn. July is the month with the longest and sunniest days of the year. It would seem that Nature encouraged conception in July so that babies would be born in April, when the weather is mild, giving them a much better chance of survival.

Why Do Some Herbalists Recommend Eating Pumpkin Seeds?

The prostate gland contains 10 times the zinc found in most other organs of the body. Pumpkin seeds have a very high zinc content, as well as magnesium, iron, phosphorus, calcium, Vitamin A and the B vitamins together with unsaturated fatty acids. They are a good, nutritious source of many healthful things that contribute to the overall well-being, as well as providing the vitamins and minerals that might be missing in the daily diet.

Some herbalists recommend that half a cup of unsalted, shelled pumpkin seeds be eaten daily.

What Gemstone Is Associated With Sexual Energy?

Rubies are thought to contribute to sexual energy. For those interested in crystals and gem therapy, a raw ruby crystal makes an interesting and fairly inexpensive piece of jewellery.

What Is An Aphrodisiac?

Named after the Greek goddess of love, Aphrodite, who had a number of lovers, including the handsome and desirable Adonis; any substance which arouses the sexual instinct is an aphrodisiac. Originally given to the woman to increase her desire for a particular man or to assure that she would be interested in no one else, the meaning has now been expanded to include any substance which not only increases desire but increases sexual energy, encourages and maintains the erection, intensifies orgasm or enhances the enjoyment of sex.

One of the most powerful reasons for the belief in aphrodisiacs is the hope that they may act as a rejuvenator for those whose potency has declined and increase their ability to sustain sexual performance. The difficulty is that there does not seem to be any substance which can stimulate or affect the highly complicated hormonal response in the human. Most so-called aphrodisiacs either increase blood flow or cause an irritation to the sexual organs. Others can affect the special chemical messengers that transmit electrical stimulation of the nervous system. Completion of the transmission of these messages depends on a chemical called dopamine and the reduction of this system is controlled by another chemical named serotonin. Anything that would increase the amount of dopamine or decrease the supply of serotonin would theoretically increase desire. Modern chemicals, some of them in use in psychiatry, affect the levels of dopamine in the brain.

There are numerous purported aphrodisiacs and from time immemorial men and women, scientists and sorcerers have brewed all kinds of love potions and aphrodisiacs.

All medicinal plants and herbs contain chemicals which will affect the human body in some manner. While most of them, such as ginseng, damiana and gotu-kola are beneficial, others are harmful and can cause health problems when used in excess.

Most of these potions, while they have some actual physiological effects on the human body, rely on magic and the universal wish for a cure, the need to believe that 'something' will somehow magically solve the problem. When the thought is held strongly enough that a medication or a herb, or an amulet will help, these beliefs can become a physiological reality.

This effect, known as the placebo effect, works only because the recipients so strongly believe that they are being helped. Even if there is no scientific evidence to support their belief in the beneficial effects. The power of suggestion can be very powerful. Additionally, there is some evidence that these powerful expectations that the love potion will make a change, can cause the release of some chemicals, such as endorphins, which do actually create changes in the brain.

There are four categories of aphrodisiacs:

1. **Activators** – substances which increase the desire for sex, usually by removing inhibitions. Alcohol falls into this category.
2. **Rejuvenators** – substances that renew the sexual abilities of youth.
3. **Prolongers** – substances that make it possible to sustain erections for a greater period of time.
4. **Amplifiers** – substances that increase sensations and heighten and intensify orgasm.

For all the claimed successes of the thousands of things that have been considered aphrodisiacs over the centuries, they all worked in only one of three ways:

1. **Nutrition** – the substance was effective for the individual man using it because it supplied his body with some basic essential nutrient he was lacking. This can explain why some things were effective for one man and not another.
2. **Irritation** – there were chemicals in the substance that were irritating to the tissues of the urethra or the mucous membranes, causing the person to be acutely aware of them as they became either irritated or itchy.
3. **Placebo** – the substance had some kind of 'magical' property that the man (or woman) was willing to believe in with sufficiently powerful thinking that it was able to affect their belief system enough to overcome some previously held limiting thinking. One of the most powerful demonstrations of this kind of 'mind over matter' is when a 'miracle' cure takes place for someone – a person who has been on crutches for years is able to throw them away in one instance of tremendously powerful belief in an external force.

How Did Some Things Become Thought Of As Aphrodisiacs?

The first aphrodisiacs were based on food and most of them in their natural state resembled either the sexual organs or possessed an odour that resembled that emanating from the sex organs. The ancient Greeks and Romans for instance, drank a liquid made from an orchid whose bulbs were shaped like testicles.

The mandrake was another plant whose shape was human and whose magical powers were most sought after. It was believed that the mandrake grew on sites where men had been hanged and these primitive people believed that the hanged man ejaculated with his last gasp. They thought that the sperm took root beneath the gallows and there produced the mandrake. Mandrakes were said to possess the animal-like capacity of uttering a cry when pulled from the earth, and it was also believed they could cause death or madness to any person extracting them from the ground. To escape this danger people tied one end of a string around the mandrake and attached the other end to a dog's tail so that the plant could be uprooted by the dog as it ran away. Despite the fear of the power of the root, or perhaps because of its awesome reputed power, it was sought after to bring fecundity to sterile women and potency to men. Mandrake contains such powerful alkaloids as scopalamine, atropine and hyoscyamine, all of which probably removed all sexual inhibitions. It was often used to spike the wines at Greek and Roman orgies and was added to the caldrons in which witches of the Middle Ages brewed their various concoctions for love potions. Since its ingredients created unpredictable reactions, it may have contributed to the wild and uninhibited behaviour of those who were given it to drink.

In the Middle Ages, garlic, radishes, turnips and onions, all testicle-shaped vegetables, were recommended. Those wanting to father a child ate fruits with lots of seeds, such as pomegranate, figs or tomatoes – then called a love apple.

When these substances failed to have an effect on increasing erections, animal parts with a clearly symbolic association with power and strength, such as the rhino horn and powdered reindeer antler, became popular. The rhino horn, which is actually compacted hair and not a horn at all, made its way into the aphrodisiac beliefs of the Orientals and so many rhinos were killed for their horn that rhinos have almost become extinct. Some societies believed that the eating of the sex organs of animals, such as stewed bull and dog testicles, or dried animal penises, would empower the man with the hormones, sex drive and potency of these creatures.

The oyster is a famed aphrodisiac and researchers believe that its shape, similar to the testicle, as well as its odour, which is thought to be similar to the odour of ejaculate, are the origins of its claimed aphrodisiacal properties.

It is possible that some of the foodstuffs for which these almost magical powers were claimed, did contribute to an overall improvement in the nutritional state (such as the high levels of zinc in the oyster). When they were effective in restoring potency, it was possibly a combination of the placebo effect and the additional essential nutrition of providing some lacking vitamins and minerals in the diets of those who claimed they had worked for them.

Because sometimes something works for one man, he tells another. In addition, belief and trust in the individual providing the aphrodisiac and an enormous need to believe in an erotic fantasy may sometimes cause a placebo to be effective.

What Are Alkaloids?

One of a large group of organic, basic substances found in plants, alkaloids are found in many of the things thought of as aphrodisiacs. Alkaloids – such as caffeine, nicotine, morphine and strychnine – are usually bitter in taste and physiologically active.

How Long Have Men Used Aphrodisiacs?

The plants that are considered to be aphrodisiacs existed long before the first human appeared on earth. No one knows how long it took for humans to discover that certain plants had properties that affected body chemistry, but sites in Iraq show that the Neanderthals used various herbs for treatments as early as 60,000 years ago. Prehistoric humans probably noticed that when animals were ill they would often eat plants they ordinarily ignored. Our ancestors may have sampled these plants and noticed that they had effects on their wakefulness and sleepiness, and were laxatives or diuretics. Effective herbs were incorporated into prehistoric shamanism and later into today's medicine.

Why Is Chocolate Considered An Aphrodisiac?

St Valentine, an early Christian martyr, is commonly regarded as the patron saint of lovers. Saint Valentine's day is observed on 14th February, the day Saint Valentine was martyred and it is a day on which lovers traditionally exchange affectionate messages and gifts, often a heart-shaped box of chocolates, elaborately decorated with lace and satin ribbons. The sending of these love notes and gifts of sweets arose in the late Middle Ages and it probably relates to the medieval European belief that birds began to mate on that date, just at the beginning of spring.

Cocoa contains the amino acid phenylethylamine and is rich in phosphorus, a mineral necessary for an erection. It also has a rather potent stimulant, theobromine.

Montezuma, the last Aztec emperor of Mexico, made a love brew with powdered cocoa boiled with honey and vanilla. When adventurers and explorers came to the New World, they discovered Montezuma's sweet love candy and when they returned from the New World, they took cocoa back to Europe with them as an aphrodisiac.

When sugar was added to the aphrodisiac mixture, chocolate sweets became a very appropriate gift to give to the one you loved and wanted to love you. Probably, the tradition evolved because the aphrodisiac content of the sweet gift was thought likely to stimulate loving feelings in the recipient.

Is Alcohol An Aphrodisiac?

Alcohol often removes inhibitions. People will get up and sing and dance and behave in a boisterous manner after drinking who would never have considered performing in such a manner without it. But, in fact, chemically alcohol is a depressant and its effects are very dose-dependent. Take too much and the euphoric effects soon fade, leaving the individual with the opposite effect.

Why Are Some Street Drugs Considered Aphrodisiacs?

Cannabis sativa, commonly known as marijuana, removes inhibitions in a manner similar to alcohol. Masters and Johnson, in their studies, found that it relaxes the musculature, making the individual feel loose and free, increases the sensitivity of the skin and increases the intensity of orgasm.

However, just like alcohol, its effects are dose-dependent and it can have the opposite effect in that it eventually suppresses the sex drive.

Cocaine, mescaline, LSD and amyl nitrate all affect sexual desire by altering the levels of brain chemicals. However, all these chemicals are dose, timing and social context related and ultimately require regularly increasing dosages and create an eventual dependency to achieve sexual satisfaction.

What Are The Four Major Herbal Traditions For The Preparation Of Aphrodisiacs?

1: Chinese; 2: Ayuravedic (India); 3: European (including Egyptian); 4: American Indian.

For thousands of years, Old World cultures were isolated from the Americas. However, when the cultures finally met, they found that they were using many of the same herbs for the same reasons. These traditions of herbal medicine included hundreds, perhaps thousands of treatments for impotence and all of them provided aphrodisiacs.

How Does Ayuravedic Medicine Work On Impotence?

India's herbal tradition is almost as old as China's. They call their herbal medicine 'Ayuraveda', meaning 'life' and 'knowledge'. The 4,500-year-old Rig Veda contains formulas for medicines using 67 herbs including ginger, cinnamon and senna and combines herbal remedies to bring a man to full vitality for life.

The Ayuravedic physician would carefully examine the patient and prescribe a combination of herbs, carefully calculated to improve the nutrition, provide restful sleep and aid the body in healing.

How Did The European Herbal Tradition Work?

In 1874 in the Valley of the Tombs, a German found the world's oldest surviving medical text, dating from 1500 B.C. It summarised more than 1,000 years of ancient Egyptian medicine and listed 876 herbal formulas made from more than 500 plants. By 500 B.C. Egyptian herbalists were considered the finest in the Mediterranean and emperors from Rome to Babylon sought their advice. Aspiring European physicians who went to Egypt to study began to influence European medicine. They brought back to Europe the things they had learned and began to do away with some of the then popular practices such as bleeding and leeches. Some of the ideas they brought back are valid today. For example: they bandaged mouldy bread over wounds (modern antibiotics are derived from moulds); they believed garlic and onion strengthened the body and prevented disease (a view presently held by modern science).

Why Is The Chinese Tradition So Strong In The Treatment Of Impotence?

The origins of Chinese herbalism are lost in the mists of time, but legend has it that around 3400 B.C., a wise man, Shen Nung, discovered that many plants had medicinal value. He tested herbs on himself, recorded their effects and died after consuming too much of one that was poisonous. This wise man (wise, up until that fatal dose!) composed many herbal prescriptions using dozens of herbs, including rhubarb and opium poppy. Succeeding emperors ordered new herbal remedies and in 1590 a herbalist published a catalogue, listing 1,094 medicinal plants and 11,000 herbal formulas.

These Chinese formulas operate on the premise that each organ of the body must function properly and in harmony with all the others in order to create optimal health; that specific herbs have a natural affinity for specific organs and glands and are important for toning these organs and tissues, to bring them into balance. Since they believe that the body is yin (internal and soft) and yang (external and hard), you cannot simply take one herb or one formula, but need to balance the yin and yang for the body to be in harmony. All Chinese aphrodisiac formulas are considered yang tonics and are used in balancing yang deficiencies. Chinese herbalists believe that until the body is properly balanced, there is no health and impotence cannot be cured.

What Is One Oriental Remedy Anyone Can Try?

An Oriental remedy, one recommended by Japanese herbalists and acupuncturists, is to squeeze the testicles gently every day, one squeeze for each year of life.

Why Do The Japanese And Many Other Orientals Believe In Ginseng For Treating Impotence?

There are three different ginsengs: Chinese or Korean, American and Siberian. Ginseng contains a mixture of several glycosides and is a very volatile oil. It stimulates the heart and internal secretions and increases muscle tone. It has an anticlotting effect and reduces blood sugar levels, both beneficial in the treatment of impotence.

Several studies have attempted to investigate the ancient Chinese belief that ginseng is a sexual stimulant. One study showed that ginseng-treated experimental animals became more sexually active than others.

Ginseng is a natural herb in which the appearance is very human and this appearance may have been the reason it was used in the first place. But it has proven itself effective based on its chemical content and has been used by the Japanese and other Orientals for centuries to treat impotence. It comes in tablets, capsules, powder extract and the whole root and is readily obtainable almost everywhere in the world. Most herbalists think that eating a small slice of the whole root every day is the most beneficial way to take ginseng.

What Other Aphrodisiacs Do The Chinese Regularly Recommend?

The Chinese recommend a great variety of herbs and other treatments, including powdered deer antler, rhino horn and acupuncture.

However, one herb they particularly favour is *ginkgo biloba,* from a tree native to eastern China. This herb interferes with the action of a substance the body produces called platelet activation factor. By inhibiting this PAF, it has enormous healing potential, particularly in arterial blood flow, internal blood clots and some strokes. As men grow older, blood flow to the brain can decrease and that means less nutrients and oxygen for brain cells. If blood flow becomes blocked, the result is a stroke. Dozens of studies show ginkgo significantly increases blood flow to all areas of the body, including the flow to the penis.

In a recent study, it was shown to aid in relieving impotence caused by narrowing of the arteries that supply blood to the penis. This herb is available in capsule form from any health food store. If purchased in leaf form, it is brewed into a tea and taken daily.

Gotu kola is another herb the Chinese like for impotence, which contains up to 3.5 per cent caffeine and 1 per cent theobromine. Both these alkaloids are noted for their central nervous system stimulation and diuretic action. These alkaloids are also thought to rejuvenate the nerves, brain and endocrine glands.

Some Oriental herbalists suggest that gotu kola be taken with ginseng. It is usually made into a tea by infusing half a teaspoonful in a cup of hot water.

What Are Some Of The Combinations Of Aphrodisiacs That The Chinese Use?

The Chinese herbal tradition is centuries old. Over the years various herbalists have worked with a variety of combinations, some of them with exotic names. One is the *male silkworm moth tonic.* This contains the actual moth, ginseng, dried dog penis, dried deer penis and some other herbs, all in a capsule.

Another tonic is the *sea horse fish nourishing tablet.* It contains dried sea horse, dried sheep penis, ginseng, cinnamon bark, various leaves and rhizomes, ginger and other various ingredients.

Still another is the *male treasure capsule,* which contains an interesting variety of ingredients, including donkey-skin glue, dried dog kidney, deer horn and sea horse, among other things.

It is quite possible that the active ingredients are the various nutritional factors, such as provided by the herbal ingredients and the rare and hard-to-get exotic ingredients have a powerful placebo effect.

What Aphrodisiac Is Recommended In Sri Lanka?

Native herbalists noticed that elephants, renowned for their longevity, love the gotu kola leaves. There is an old Sinhalese proverb which advises,

"Take two leaves a day, keep old age away."

Gotu kola has been known to improve circulation to the lower extremities, which may account for its being touted as an aphrodisiac.

In Mexico, What Aphrodisiac Is Recommended For Lovers?

Damiana, whose leaves contain a mildly irritating oil which is excreted in the urine, is considered an aphrodisiac, as well as a tonic for the nervous system. It may be the irritating effect which is responsible for damiana being considered an aphrodisiac. Even the Aztecs thought it was a sexual stimulant and a cure for impotence and it is considered a remedy for performance anxiety.

The Mexicans take a teaspoonful of the leaves of this plant and add it to a cup of boiling water, allow it to steep for 10 minutes, then strain and drink this tea daily before breakfast.

Many livestock breeders in Mexico use it to stimulate their studs for breeding.

In Ecuador, What Aphrodisiac Is Recommended For A Flagging Interest In Sex?

Ecuadoreans enjoy a tea made from the seeds of the *guarana,* a local herb. The seeds are gathered in the autumn and crushed, mixed into a paste with water, formed into sticks and dried over a fire. Ecuadoreans grate a bit of this stick into a cup of boiling water and make a very stimulating tea.

Its aphrodisiac action may be attributed to the fact that it contains twice as much caffeine as coffee.

In The South Pacific, What Is Recommended To Assist One's Sex Life?

Kava kava, a perennial shrub is found on the islands of the South Pacific. This herb contains alkaloids that produce drowsiness. It is recommended as a sedative, to combat both anxiety and fatigue. It is thought to produce a relaxed, euphoric state without affecting the ability to think.

The people of the South Pacific chew the root of this herb, because it is not water soluble and cannot be brewed into any kind of a beverage. It is thought to affect the spinal nerves to produce a gentle warmth as the genitals are engorged with blood.

Kava kava oil is also applied directly to the glans of the penis and is thought to generate a tingling to the nerve endings there.

In The Philippines, What Is Recommended To Spice Up One's Love Life?

The *dita tree* which is found throughout the Philippines and Southeast Asia, produces a bitter seed which is used to brew a tea.

The seeds contain a potent alkaloid, known as chlorogenine, or alstonine. This bitter tea is thought to stimulate erections and prevent premature ejaculation.

The people of the Philippines crush the seeds and soak them in water overnight. The liquid is strained and made into a drink the next day.

What Do East Indians Recommend To Heat Up One's Potency?

An *eggplant dish* cooked with butter and chives and then covered with a very hot, very spicy curry sauce is eaten daily.

Another widely acclaimed potion is ram's testicles boiled in milk and sugar and eaten before bedtime.

What Do German Love Experts Recommend?

They suggest drinking honey-beer for 30 days. One ounce of hops is placed in a porcelain container covered with a pint of boiling water and allowed to stand for 15 minutes.

After straining, the Germans add a teaspoonful of raw honey to a wineglassful of tea and drink this beverage one hour before each meal. The honey contains aspartic acid and Vitamin E, both of which contribute to general health and well-being.

What Do The Great Lovers In Turkey Recommend?

Turks drink a cup of *fenugreek tea* daily, prepared with two teaspoonfuls of fenugreek seeds in a cup of just-boiled water. They steep this drink for five minutes, strain and add honey and lemon to taste. They suggest drinking one cup daily. Fenugreek contains Vitamin A and trimethlamine, as well as a strong-smelling bitter oil and the alkaloids choline and trigoneline. This oil is irritating to mucous membranes and has a strong disagreeable odour and bitter taste; the lemon probably disguises the odour and the honey covers the bitter taste.

What Aphrodisiac Do American Indians Recommend To Improve Virility?

Europeans, who considered American Indians ignorant savages except when it came to health and healing were amazed at the good health, physical stamina and fine teeth of these people. Some Europeans studied Indian medicine, particularly that of those tribes they found on the Eastern coast of the USA. Many were cured with the Indians' traditional medicine and with herbs such as American ginseng or had a fever treated in the Indian sweat lodges.

A traditional American Indian treatment for impotence is to add two tablespoonfuls of unrefined oatmeal and half a cup of raisins to one quart of water and bring this mixture to a boil. Reduce the heat, cover and simmer slowly for 45 minutes. After removing from the heat, strain and add the juice of two lemons and honey to taste. They recommend drinking one cup before breakfast and another one hour before bedtime. Oatmeal is rich in Vitamin E and honey contains many vitamins and minerals, as well as including hormones.

What Love Potion Did The American Cowboys Use Without Realising It?

Cowboys drank *sarsaparilla,* believing it a treatment for syphilis; it was the most widely used treatment for this sexually-transmitted disease during the 19th century. After a visit to the local brothel, they would head for the nearest saloon and order some sarsaparilla.

The Caribbean and North American Indians also used it to treat urinary complaints and as a tonic to keep one young and vigorous, both physically and sexually. Sarsaparilla is a sweet-tasting root and was used as a flavouring agent in a drink now known as root beer. Made from the dried root of the climbing vine which grows easily in tropical America, it was thought to contain the male hormone testosterone, as well as progesterone and cirtin, an adrenal hormone. What it does contain is some saponins which bear a chemical resemblance to testosterone. When made into a tea or a cool beverage and drunk in sufficient quantities, it may have had some stimulating effect on the libido. While the cowboy was not curing his sexually-transmitted disease, he was probably increasing his desire to return to the brothel.

What Aphrodisiac Does The British Tradition Recommend?

Since the early British physicians studied in Egypt, their aphrodisiac tradition is based on the thinking of that culture. They suggest combining one ounce of liquorice root with two teaspoonfuls of crushed fennel seed and two cups of water. This is brought to a boil, covered and simmered slowly for 20 minutes. Cool, strain and bottle it. Believers in this remedy drink one to three tablespoonfuls twice a day.

What Did The Ancient Druids Recommend?

These wise men of long ago mixed two level tablespoonfuls of milk and water, a quarter of a teaspoonful of powdered ginger, an eighth of a teaspoonful of powdered cinnamon, four tablespoonfuls of raw honey and a dash of lemon juice, plus any fresh fruit available. They drank this mixture half an hour before bedtime.

What Can Actually Increase Sexual Desire?

Chemical messengers in the brain transmit messages to the nerves in a complex system of electrical circuitry.

The chemical messenger that increases desire is called dopamine and the one that decreases desire is named serotonin. Some foods are sources of serotonin and are taken as a calmer or tranquilliser. This is why people who have difficulty falling asleep may often drink a mug of warm milk at bedtime.

Many of the so-called modern aphrodisiacs work by altering the balance of these two chemicals in the brain. Some of the medicines currently in use in psychiatry have an effect on these two chemical messengers and are effective in either reducing or increasing one or the other.

Anything that increases the amount of dopamine or decreases the serotonin should increase sexual desire.

Is There Anything That Has Not Been Considered An Aphrodisiac At One Time Or Another?

Probably not. Over the centuries mankind has tried almost anything and everything; every plant, herb, insect, animal part or combination thereof which we could imagine including some which seem laughable to modern man. Ideas such as rubbing your body with a topaz which had been soaked in wine, eating bat wings, desiccated sea horse or dried dog penis, all of which seem incredibly silly today, were once accepted as part of the healing practices of ancient times.

At some time during the 14th century, the image of the folk herbalist changed from being wise and magical to someone involved with the devil and performing witchcraft. The practice of herbal medicine and the creating of healing mixtures, cosmetics, love potions and aphrodisiacs became associated with evil spells and poison. At the same time, when the 'regular' physicians, who looked down on the folk healers as ignorant practitioners of inferior medicine, relied on bleeding, violent laxatives and mercury to cure most things, including impotence.

Eventually, scientists experimented with herbs, analysed them chemically, extracted their active constituents and published their findings in scientific journals for all to explore, study and understand. That science has become the basis for the pharmacy of scientifically-grounded medicine which is practised today. Herbs and foodstuffs are the forgotten sources of many of the medicines we now use, many of which synthetically duplicate the form found in nature. However, a lot of what the ancients practised was almost universal among the four great herbal traditions.

What Is One Of The Most Celebrated Herbs For The Treatment Of Impotence?

Liquorice root was used by all of the traditions and its effects come from the 150 chemicals it contains, one of which is the hormone oestrogen. More than 5,000 years ago, the first great Chinese herbal documents listed it and it has been a worldwide favourite for a variety of ailments, although it has many side-effects, some of them quite dangerous. One of its major assets was that it masked the bitter flavour of other herbs. (The liquorice candy sold today is made from star anise and is not liquorice root at all.)

Liquorice root as a treatment for impotence is made by boiling the root in water until it thickens. It is then mixed with milk and sweetened with honey and taken daily.

Should You Try An Aphrodisiac?

Some aphrodisiacs are totally harmless and some have some rather unpleasant side-effects. Be aware that they work by one of the three means listed and are probably not effective over the long-term. Also, they might prevent you from getting proper treatment and delay finding the cause of the dysfunction longer, making it more difficult to treat.

If you decide you would like to try one of these, get some advice from a reliable herb shop about the contents of the products you are purchasing and the side-effects to be on the look out for. Maybe just consider the experiment as just that, a fun experiment – and then get serious with finding a proper diagnosis.

4 How Can Impotence Be Treated Or Cured?

NINETY-SEVEN PER CENT OF PROBLEMS OF POTENCY CAN BE TREATED OR CURED!

As you are reading this, there is already a treatment that is applicable to your potency problem and with proper diagnosis, you can be on your way to renewed potency now!

We have already learned that in order to be potent, have an erection that can be sustained for enough time to have intercourse to orgasm, three things are necessary:

1. There must be a blood supply to the penis that is sufficient to inflate the two balloon-like structures of the penis to rigidity and keep that blood there until orgasm. The penis is an organ without any supporting parts that would contribute to its firmness and it must rely entirely on the blood that fills it to be adequate for insertion.
2. There must be adequate nerve function to respond to sexual stimulation, get the various arteries to open up, allow the blood to enter the two chambers of the penis and then remain there long enough for intercourse to take place.
3. There must be an adequate veinous system to keep that blood within the penis with sufficient stability to maintain the erection.

Without any one of these three factors, potency will be a problem and it is difficult without a medical examination to know just what the difficulty is. Obviously, at that point a thorough medical examination is usually needed to determine the reason for the loss of potency and decide what must be done to regain erectile functioning and a return to a life of love.

Ninety-seven per cent of problems with erectile function can be treated and cured with medication, changes in life-style, surgery and/or psychological counselling.

Ninety-seven per cent!

That means that almost everyone can find a solution.

The answer is up to you!!

Is There A Way A Man Can Test For Potency At Home?

Most men have five to six erections while they sleep, and these erections coincide with periods of REM sleep. Men often wake up in the morning with an erection. These erections occur when all the physical structures are operating properly, no matter how uptight, stressed out or otherwise impotent these men might be while awake.

To test whether or not these nightly erections occur, purchase a strip of postage stamps or similar. At bedtime, wrap a single thickness of stamps around the shaft of the penis. Stick the first and last stamps together, overlapping each other.

When a night-time erection occurs, and the circumference of the penis increases, the stamps should break along the line of one of the perforations. If the impotence is caused by something organically wrong, the man will awaken with the strip of stamps intact. Repeat this test nightly for a week or two, in case the stamps have been torn when turning over during the night.

If the stamps are regularly broken along the perforation the chances are that there is a normal capacity for erections and the cause of the impotency is probably psychological. Sometimes it is a great relief to find out that the impotence is caused by something physically wrong, something that can be treated. Sometimes it is just as great a relief to find out that the cause is psychological, because this can be altered also, by changes in thinking about stressful problems or through work with a therapist who specialises in sexual difficulties. This stamp test is a starting point for discovering the cause of the impotence and just may give a man the courage to begin to look for the causative factors, instead of simply agonising over the loss of potency.

If A Man Decides To Go To The Doctor, What Kinds Of Questions Will Be Asked And What Will The Examination Be Like?

The doctor will take a complete medical history: What kinds of medications do you take for other medical conditions, what illnesses have you had in the past, what injuries? It is best to tell the doctor everything, even if it seems minor. Sometimes the medications for other things, such as high blood pressure, can cause impotence and there are other medications that can be substituted. Sometimes past injuries, long forgotten, such as a straddle injury sustained many years ago, can cause damage to the nerves that has not shown up until the present. The portion of the penis known as the crus is often the site of injuries such as straddle injuries and cyclists can sometimes have problems with potency simply because the constant sitting on the bicycle seat creates pressure on the erection nerves. The doctor will ask questions such as, "Do you find that you have to shave less frequently?" "Do you ever have hot flushes?" If the answers to these questions is, "Yes," that could indicate an insufficient level of hormones, easily treated by replacement. "How much do you smoke?" "How much alcohol do you consume daily?" "Do you use cocaine, other recreational drugs?" "Do you take medications for your heart or ulcers?" The answers to these questions all offer clues to the experienced physician.

The doctor will also take a sexual history; this is the only way he can evaluate in what way the erections have changed. Only the patient can tell him if the erections are different from how they used to be. He will ask questions like, "Do you sometimes wake up with an erection?" "Do you have impotence only in specific situations or with a specific partner?" The situation of specific impotence is a very telling clue. It might be that the patient is feeling guilt or anger and some change in dealing with either or both of those emotions might be necessary to treat the condition. "Does it take longer to get an erection than it did, say three years ago, one year ago, one month ago?" "Are you able to masturbate but not have intercourse?" This is all essential information and the answers will indicate ways to rule out a number of problems.

The doctor will examine the penis and testicles, he will test the penis's pulse, and check its blood pressure. The blood pressure is taken by a miniature version of the cuff used around the arm. The cavernosal arteries – the erection arteries – run through each of the corpus cavernosum (the erectile chambers). These arteries are about 0.6 millimeters in diameter and the blood flowing through them should be at the same pressure as the arteries in your arm. That is, approximately 120/80. The top number, the 120 is the maximum pressure in the artery, when blood is coursing through it. The lower number is the minimum pressure of the artery. However, the blood pressures within the erection chambers themselves are usually written with one number. Pressure inside the erection chambers, not the arteries that supply them, show the maximum arterial pressure during erection, less the pressure lost through blood draining out by the veins during an erection. The normal pressure inside an erection chamber is approximately 90. This is the pressure of the blood flow in of 120, less the pressure lost as blood flows out. If this internal penis pressure is at variance with the normal figure, then the doctor has another clue as to what avenue to explore, looking for the cause of the dysfunction.

The doctor will examine the testicles, the penis itself and the scrotum, looking to see if they all seem normal, have not atrophied or appear to be diseased in any other manner.

A blood test will follow, looking for anything that might indicate a deficiency in any hormones that are necessary for potency. Cholesterol levels will be checked to indicate any need for dietary changes or if medication might be needed to bring cholesterol under control. Finally, a urinalysis will check for blood sugar levels, as diabetes often goes undiscovered until the impotence occurs.

What Is Necessary For A Man To Be Considered In Need Of Treatment For Impotence?

The individual going to the doctor for treatment of impotence should find that changes in his erections (rigidity or sustaining capability or both) occur with morning erections, during masturbation and during intercourse for a period of six months.

What Other Tests Might The Doctor Use?

One follow-up test that might be performed is the DICC Study. This is an abbreviation for 'dynamic infusion cavernosometry and cavernosography'. This is a four-part examination of the erectile system during a drug-induced erection.

The study begins when the physician injects a large dose of a combination of papaverine and pentolamine into the erectile chambers of the penis. Papaverine relaxes the smooth-muscle tissue of the erectile chambers and penile arteries. Pentolamine blocks the constriction of smooth-muscle tissue and arteries that can be generated by the patient's own hormone adrenaline and its neurotransmitter noradrenaline. These chemicals are released by the endocrine system when the patient is anxious.

The first part of the study records the blood pressure response within the erectile chambers of the penis following injection. The doctor discovers how close the penile blood pressure approaches the patient's regular pressure in the artery of his arm.

The second part of this study tests the blood storage mechanism by infusing a saline solution into the erection chambers until the penis reaches a pre-defined pressure. The doctor then records how fast the erection pressure falls after the infusion of the saline is terminated. The normal storage mechanism is very efficient and the flow of the saline needed to maintain pressure and the drop in erection pressure is usually very small. If the storage mechanism is not functioning properly, there will be a high flow of saline needed to maintain pressure in the erection chambers or a marked drop in the pressure when the saline infusion is stopped.

The third part of this study uses ultrasound to measure the blood pressure in the penile arteries to see if the pressure is adequate.

The fourth and final part of the study, the cavernosography, is an X-ray of the erect penis, providing the physician with valuable anatomical information regarding the storage mechanism of the penis.

This DICC study is invaluable in diagnosing the problems of potency as it provides information that was unavailable just a few short years ago. It gives doctors the ability actually to examine all the internal structures of the penis and pinpoint the areas where the trouble might lie, and indicate ways to cure the dysfunction.

What Is A Rigiscan Monitor?

A monitor that measures the increase in circumference of the penis upon erection, and its degree of rigidity as well. This monitoring is usually done in a sleep laboratory and is sometimes performed when the possibility of psychogenic impotence is considered.

What Is Cavernosography And Cavernosometry?

When the effectiveness of the veins that trap the blood can be tested by infusing a contrast media or dye into the penis and visualising it by fluoroscope. At the same time, the pressures and volumes of fluids needed to fill the penis are measured. This test evaluates the valve mechanism, the patency and number of veins that are not closing off properly and discloses whether or not a relatively simple procedure in which the veins are tied off will be successful.

What Is A Bulbocavernous Reflex Latency Text?

This test identifies neurologic damage to the muscle at the base of the urethra which contracts during erection. This test will indicate whether or not the nerves that cause it to constrict and are necessary for an erection, are functioning. The penis is injected with erection-causing drugs and will indicate to the doctor not only whether or not these nerves have been damaged but the degree of damage and whether or not a sufficient arterial flow is still possible.

What Is An Arteriogram?

An X-ray of the arteries leading to and inside the penis is performed in the erect state under sedation. Novocaine is injected into the skin of the patient's groin. A small tube is introduced through the anaesthetised skin into an artery of the leg and on through to the artery in the erectile chamber. At present it is performed on those patients who wish to consider vascular reconstructive surgery and who, after a DICC study, demonstrate low blood pressure in the erection artery as well as an absence of any of the multiple blood storage problems.

If The Problem Is Failure To Fill, What Can Be Done?

Failure to fill can be caused by arterial blockages due to atherosclerosis, ageing or injury. After tests to determine just where the problem lies, whether in the arteries, in the nerves or in the veins, a suitable treatment can be selected.

If The Problem Is Atherosclerosis Of The Arteries, What Can Be Done?

There are operations to remove the fat from the arteries leading to the heart, as well as operations to bypass these same arteries to the heart. Sometimes the removal of this fatty plaque is possible but if the arterial wall is scarred and hardened and if the artery has narrowed, then revascularisation surgery, known as arterial bypass surgery, can be done. This involves re-routeing a healthy artery to the penis to bring a reliable supply of high pressure blood to it. The surgeon grafts sections of an abdominal artery around narrowed branches of the main artery leading to the penis.

What Are The Advantages Of Revascularisation Surgery?

If the surgery is successful, the man will have natural erections again. The success rate is between 30 and 80 per cent. The younger the man, the higher the rate of success.

What Are The Disadvantages Of Revascularisation Surgery?

The surgeon may not find there are any normal arteries to work with. Also, many men are eliminated as candidates for this surgery. Smokers, for instance, are ruled out because nicotine sends the new artery into spasms and the man would soon be impotent again. Other medical conditions may also make some men poor risks.

Frequently, after a couple of years, these same arteries become clogged again and the bypass surgery is no longer good. Why? Well the answer lies in what clogs these arteries in the first place and the answer to that is fat: excessive fat in the diet. If the arteriosclerosis is systemic, that is to say, all throughout the body, it seems reasonable that this arteriosclerosis would apply to the arteries of the penis as well. The penis has no other means of support; no bones, no tendons, no ligaments. It must rely completely on an adequate blood supply to make it firm, therefore, the patency of these arteries is of paramount importance.

If you were to tap on a spot on the back of your hand with the point of a pencil, for several hours every day, you would eventually develop a sore. It would not matter if you applied all the healing creams in the world: if you continued to tap that same place with the pencil, the injury would come back. The same applies to the arteries: if they are continually filled up with fat, they will continue to develop the small fatty plaques on their internal walls, plaque that narrows them, blocks them, scars them, and keeps the blood from flowing through them. Cholesterol is a major contributor to the early development of atherosclerosis, the hardening and narrowing of the arteries.

Over a lifetime, what a man eats may have a significant effect on the arteries and the part they play in successful blood flow to the penis.

These fat-blocked arteries can be freed of this blockage by reducing the saturated fat in the diet and allowing life-giving blood, with its oxygen that feeds every cell of the body, to flow freely. This is particularly important for the man with a family history of high cholesterol or a genetic predisposition to vascular disorders. There is almost no need for saturated fat in the diet. The body can make this type of fat from other sources. A man can survive with little dietary saturated fats.

Diabetes: What Is The Most Important Single Thing To Do To Retain Potency?

CONTROL YOUR DIET!

Diabetes is the most common cause of impotence. It is not possible to consider the entire subject of diabetes in this book, but the following will give some idea of what should be done.

The diet for a diabetic is based on five factors: total calories, percentage and type of carbohydrates, percentage and type of fats, meal spacing and adjustments for exercise or complicating disorders. For most diabetics who are taking insulin, the total caloric intake should be between 1,400 and 2,700 a day, with the exact amount depending on daily activity and desired weight of the patient.

For the diabetic who is not insulin-dependent, three divided meals of approximately equal calories are recommended. The optimum diet is usually worked out by a doctor and a dietician. It may have a high fibre content, which has been found to be beneficial in diabetics.

There are dozens of excellent books that tell the reader how to make appetising meals with reduced fat and controlled sugar. It is suggested that men limit themselves to 30 to 60 grams of fat a day. This fat content control should go hand-in-hand with the doctor's recommendations for calorie control and carbohydrate balance. It is not wise to go below these recommended fat ranges because fat supplies some essential nutrients that cannot be obtained from other foods and a minimum amount is necessary for the transport of fat-soluble vitamins. Most foods list the ingredients on the packaging and an intelligent shopper can read the label to know just how much fat and carbohydrate something contains.

The risk of impotence is far too high to ignore the need for a dietary change, should one be suggested as part of the treatment. The most common death in the industrialised world today is from heart attacks. The risk factors for heart attack are the same as those for erectile dysfunction caused by atherosclerosis of the penile arteries. The risk of death by heart attack for the average man with a normal cholesterol level of 200 to 220 is as much as 50 per cent. The risk of death by heart attack for a vegetarian is only four per cent.

Newer plaque in the arteries can be removed by dietary change; in individuals who have eaten a fatty diet for most of their lives these plaques calcify and harden, lining the insides of the arteries and narrowing them. No one need to continue accumulating this killer plaque. Dietary changes that eliminate the excessive fat from the diet are all that are necessary to reverse – and sometimes, eliminate – this hazard to your sex life.

Why Is It Important To Maintain Proper Weight?

Being overweight has been linked to coronary heart disease, atherosclerosis, angina, stroke and hypertension. Obesity increases fats in the circulation, contributing to the inability to provide oxygenated blood to the penis.

Are Clogged Arteries Reversible Without Surgery?

The answer to that question is a resounding yes, but it takes a lot of work and dietary changes to accomplish it. The rewards are worth it however, in better all round health and higher potency.

What Can Be Done If The Arteries Are Scarred?

While a change in diet to prevent continued atherosclerosis will prevent further progression of the disease, if the scarring is severe, there is not much that can be done. In this case, a vacuum constriction device might be appropriate, along with sex therapy. Arterial bypass surgery could be possible, or a penile implant. An examination will tell if the blockages can either be cleared out or successfully bypassed. The results of this type of surgery for blockages to restore erections have varied from 30 to 80 per cent. Younger men usually have fewer areas of blockages than older men, whose arterial blockages may be throughout their arterial system. As a consequence, younger men generally do better with this type of surgery than do older men.

What Can Be Done If The Difficulty Is Failure To Initiate An Erection?

The inability to initiate can have several causes: nerve damage due to disease or injury, stress, anxiety and other psychological problems, as well as some hormonal disorders. Diagnostic tests can pinpoint the cause and this will determine the type of treatment needed.

What Can Be Done If There Is Nerve Damage?

The nervous system must be able to send signals to the electrical circuits that cause the penis to respond to sexual thoughts. There are many forms of illness that can permanently damage these electrical circuits, such as a prolapsed disc, various operations of the pelvic organs, multiple sclerosis and injuries caused by accidents.

The nervous system is divided into the central nervous system, the brain and the spinal cord and the peripheral nervous system. They form a complex bundle of fibres and receptors that transmit information and commands between the central nervous system and distant parts of the body.

The peripheral nervous system contains the autonomic nervous system that controls the automatic functions of the body. You are able to breathe, your heart pumps and your digestion functions whether or not you give it any conscious instructions to do so. The ability to have an erection and to experience an orgasm are also controlled by this same autonomic nervous system.

This autonomic nervous system has two further branches, the sympathetic and parasympathetic system. Emotions determine which branch of the autonomic system is in control at any given time. When the human being feels threatened and must decide whether to fight or to run, the so-called 'flight or fight' mechanism, the body is under the control of the sympathetic system. When we are calm and relaxed, the parasympathetic system is running the show. These two systems counterbalance each other and they cannot both be in control at the same time; either one or the other is in control at any given moment.

The nerves that tell the penis to become erect are part of the parasympathetic system and the nerves that tell the penis to become flaccid are under the control of the sympathetic system. The interaction of these two sets of nerves are necessary for an erection to occur and for the subsequent detumescence to occur. These nerves release chemicals called neurotransmitters. The sympathetic nerves release neurotransmitters that keep the smooth muscle in a state of contraction, restricting blood flow into the erectile chambers. When a man becomes stimulated sexually, the spinal cord sends a signal through the parasympathetic nerves. These nerves release neurotransmitters that act to relax the muscles that restrict blood flow, allowing the penis to become filled with blood so that it might become erect.

In addition, the cells which line the spaces in these chambers release chemical agents that help relax or constrict these muscles.

Later, after ejaculation, or the cessation of sexual stimulation, the sympathetic nerves once again send out constricting neurotransmitters to close off the blood flow to the penis.

Emotions have a direct effect on whether or not these neurotransmitters are released.

There is now assistance for the chronically impotent, whose nerve damage is severe or permanent: a battery-powered suppository that elicits an erection at the push of a remote control button. This suppository enhances neurologic reflexes and stimulates nerves in the groin through the rectal wall. The custom-made Male Electronic Genital Stimulator is inserted into the rectum just before sex and is activated by a tiny remote control mechanism that fits into a wrist watch or pendant.

These battery-operated devices are undergoing clinical trials at Jefferson Medical College in Philadelphia, Pennsylvania.

What Will Vitamin E Do For Potency?

Vitamin E is considered a general tonic for sex organs. It is also an anti-oxidant and aids in the oxygenation of the tissues and is often prescribed in the treatment of impotency.

What Kind Of Muscles Are In The Penis?

The body has three different types of muscle: *skeletal*, *cardiac* and *smooth*. The penis does not contain skeletal muscle, you can't work out and get a stronger penis. Skeletal muscle is attached to bone, and this muscle can be 'worked out' and made stronger and larger. Cardiac muscle, the muscle of the heart, operates without assistance, except in times of excitement or exertion, when it responds to increased oxygen demands by pumping faster. This type of muscle can be strengthened by aerobic exercise. We can't stop hearts from beating but they can be accelerated in their pumping by thinking about threatening things.

The penis contains the third type of muscle, smooth muscle, in the walls of the tiny blood vessels known as arterioles. When arterioles relax, the supply of blood to the penis increases and the smooth-muscle walls of the erection chambers allow the lacunar spaces, where the blood is stored, to fill. The autonomic nervous system controls these smooth muscles; that is why emotions have a direct effect on the sympathetic nervous system, determining whether or not the penis will respond with an erection. Anxiety releases chemicals that keep the smooth muscle from relaxing, preventing erection.

What If The Nerves That Control Erection Have Been Affected By A Hormonal Imbalance?

The doctor can diagnose a hormonal imbalance with a simple blood test and provide the necessary hormones, perhaps testosterone or thyroid, by either injection or pill.

What If The Problem Is Low Testosterone?

An inadequate supply of testosterone will usually not cause erectile dysfunction, but it may contribute to a diminished sex drive. It is a deficiency that can readily be supplemented. Some researchers believe that since the level of testosterone can drop sharply after the age of 60, a male menopause is a reality. In tests, for men low in testosterone, supplemental testosterone increased muscle strength and sex drive, gave them more energy and stronger bones, and lowered cholesterol. But these men were known as hypogonadal and few men appear to fall into this category.

In men with normal levels of the hormone, it was found by researchers at the University of Utah that levels of the testosterone fell by 30 per cent within four hours of eating a meal containing 57 per cent fat. But hormone levels stayed the same in men who ate a meal with only two per cent fat. Obviously, this research indicates that fatty foods can contribute to a reduction in libido.

Conversely, men who had been taking anabolic steroids, primarily the hormone testosterone, in the belief that it built up muscle tissue and increased strength, were found to have adverse reactions to excessive testosterone. They had testicular atrophy, impotence and acne. The additional steroids reduced the number of disease-fighting white cells in the blood and increased their cholesterol. Long-term users were also found to have liver disorders and liver cancer.

Can Premature Ejaculation Cause Impotence?

Complex nerve impulses from the spinal centre that respond to the distension of the chamber which holds the semen are responsible for ejaculation, which usually occurs about two minutes after the start of intercourse. Nature has programmed the male to respond to this pressure in the chamber almost universally within two minutes, varying only slightly, from between ten seconds to three minutes.

Premature ejaculation becomes a problem when the man is unable to delay ejaculation long enough to satisfy his partner.

While older men are often able to delay ejaculation because of reduced sensitivity of the glans and reduced nerve response, delaying ejaculation involves suppressing a very primitive reflex.

Men are under increasing pressure to overcome this reflex and when criticised for being unable to delay, a man may begin to form an image of himself as a poor lover. Sometimes, for this reason, a sexual partner will interpret premature ejaculation as an indication that the man is indifferent to his partner's pleasure. This can become an area of conflict which can escalate if the man begins to believe he is less than other men and begins to start avoiding sex.

An anti-depression drug can be given if this is a problem causing conflict. The drug boosts the body's supply of serotonin and decreases the stimulation the man is experiencing. While the man is learning to delay, the drug aids him and after approximately six months men can cut the dosage in half and then go off the drug completely.

Does Having A Vasectomy Reversed Cure Impotence?

A vasectomy does not cause impotence and its reversal will not cure it because in neither case is the production of testosterone altered. A vasectomy is a successful method of birth control and has no effect on the production of hormones or any erectile nerves. It only prevents the sperm from ejaculating. Instead, the sperm disintegrate at the end of their normal life span and within hours white blood cells clear them out.

What Can Be Done To Help The Man With The 'Steal Syndrome'?

When the blood supply to the lower limbs and the pelvic area is severely restricted, the large-scale muscle activity at the hip that is required for intercourse in the missionary position often diverts the blood supply away from the penis, preventing an erection.

By changing from the missionary position to his back or his side and allowing the partner to be slightly over him or on top, the man can prevent this blood drain into these major muscles and keep it directed to the penis to create the necessary erection.

What If The Impotence Is Caused By Diabetes?

By age 45 more than 25 per cent of diabetic men are impotent and impotence may occur regardless of the type of treatment the man receives, whether it is by injectable insulin or oral medication. While impotence may occur early or late in life, the risk of developing impotence seems to increase the longer the diabetes exists. Better management of the diabetic patient, with strict control of the blood glucose, could result in a decline in the impotence among diabetics.

The goal of treating both Type I and Type II diabetes are essentially the same; to minimise both short- and long-term complications by normalising levels of blood sugar. Normal blood sugar is defined as falling between a low of 50mg/dl and a high of 150mg/dl. Type I diabetes requires insulin injections and matching insulin intake to diet and exercise to control blood sugar and Type II can usually be treated by diet, exercise and, if needed, drugs that increase the body's ability to utilise its insulin. Some Type I diabetics have started wearing insulin pumps, portable computerised devices that are designed to administer constant small amounts of insulin (as well as larger amounts to cover meals and other circumstances) through an indwelling needle and catheter. In Type II diabetes, treatment concentrates on increasing the natural supply of insulin and its effectiveness in the body. In 80 per cent of all Type II diabetics, diet, exercise and, if necessary, oral drugs, can control the disease. A reducing diet apparently makes the diabetic more sensitive to his own insulin and increases the amount available. The disease process of diabetes itself damages the relaxation nerves involved in the erection process and the cells that line the spaces of the erectile tissue. Diabetics are not usually good candidates for reconstructive surgery on their penile arteries and veins because of these problems with the nerves and the cells that line the erectile chambers.

But diabetics are good candidates for penile implants, and the majority of them who have had this done report excellent restoration of erectile function.

What Can Be Done For Peyronie's Disease?

Peyronie's disease is considered self-limiting: it eventually stops without treatment. When this happens, there are varying degrees of scarring of the tissue that limits the expansion of the erectile chambers. Common treatments include vitamin E, radiation therapy, anti-inflammatory medications and ultrasound. There are several surgical treatments for the removal of the scarring and filling in the resulting space with graft material or skin grafts. Sometimes a section of the tunica on the side of the penis opposite the scarring is removed, compensating for the bend. If there is a sufficient degree of curvature, sometimes a penile implant is the treatment of choice.

What If The Man Is Ageing But Otherwise In Good Health?

There is no reason a man cannot remain sexually active for as long as he desires to be active. To do so he must be aware of some of the effects that ageing have on his body. The testicles make less testosterone. The sensory nerves become less receptive to stimuli. The amount of the neurotransmitters that control smooth muscle is reduced. The arteries become athrosclerotic and the erectile tissue undergoes biochemical reactions, causing it to lose its elasticity. There are psychological changes too, a man takes longer to be stimulated and is less stimulated by physical contacts. It may be that he requires more time for fantasy and visually erotic inputs. By being aware of these physical and psychological changes, a man, as well as his partner, can then make allowances for these changes and adjust their love-making behaviour accordingly.

The older man must make changes to keep his blood pressure under control, be sure that his blood sugar does not become elevated, keep his diet low in fat, watch his cholesterol and exercise regularly. All of these things should be part of the take-charge life-style of a man who wishes to remain healthy into his old age. The kind of an old age a man has may be completely up to how he chooses to live those years. A man who wishes to maintain his ability to be sexually active with adequate erections to sustain intercourse, can and should take an active part in preventing many of these problems of ageing.

5 Updates And Advances In Treatments And Research

What Is The Treatment For Priapism?

A great number of medical conditions have been implicated in priapism: neurological disorders, herniated lumbar discs and blood diseases such as sickle-cell anaemia, leukemia and multiple myeloma. But when the storage mechanism of the penis becomes continuously activated, the priapistic erection becomes a medical emergency. The penis becomes painful as the supply of oxygenated blood to the erection chambers is cut off. Eventually, tissue begins to die. Scarring results from the damaged tissue and in many cases interferes permanently with the ability of the penis to become erect. Treatments are varied, but first the medical condition causing the problem must be identified and the blood must be drained from the penis as soon as possible.

How Do Injections Of Erection Drugs Help?

Sometimes, when there is nerve damage that is not too severe but which cannot be corrected, an erection-inducing drug can be injected into the penis to give the additional help that it needs to become erect. If the damage is too severe, a vacuum constriction device or penile implant may be the solution.

What Can Be Done If Emotions Are Preventing Erection?

The failure to initiate an erection can be caused by psychological problems and sex therapy, in conjunction with some other physical treatment is often the answer. Sex therapy can be successful only if the people involved are willing to discuss the problem openly with the therapist.

Therapists often prefer couples therapy, as most sexual problems occur within the context of a relationship. An opportunity to discuss the problems with a trained professional stranger can be particularly helpful as all the long-suppressed anger and recrimination can be defused in the discussion. Besides an extensive sexual history, the initial interview will usually include a thorough exploration of the medical history and any treatment or medication that might affect potency.

In many instances it is the sexual partner's opportunity to learn about the anatomy and physical functioning of the male, in addition to working out the relationship difficulties.

After an initial interview where the therapist learns just when and how often the impotence occurs, a dialogue can be developed that will explore the reasons for the problem.

Often it is helpful to combine psychological counselling with on-going medical procedures. When a man has problems with potency for quite a while stress can hinder medical treatment and understanding his potency problem may help him respond more quickly to his medical care.

What Can Be Done If Cancer Caused Impotence?

Cancer or its treatments can sometimes damage the nerves and blood vessels of the penis and radical surgery in the lower pelvic area can damage nerves important in the erectile process. If both testicles have been removed, there is almost a complete loss of testosterone and therefore, loss of the sex drive. Drugs for pain and chemotherapy and radiation therapy may also impair the erectile tissues. But new laser treatments are reducing the recurrence rate of prostate cancer to as low as five per cent, an indication that as techniques for early diagnosis and treatment improve, the impotence rates for these procedures will also decrease.

However, once treated for cancer, the patient who experiences erectile dysfunction should look at the problem in the same way as an individual without cancer with the same difficulties.

Cancer patients are often candidates for one of the numerous erectile assisting treatments: hormone therapy, erection-causing drugs and penile implants.

What Can Be Done About Performance Anxiety?

A man experiencing difficulty with erections should ensure a favourable sexual environment before attempting to make love. He should take the time to find a place in which he is comfortable, neither too hot or too cold, in non-threatening surroundings. He should be well-rested and interested in his partner. Fear of disease, fear of pregnancy and fear of intimacy all can inhibit arousal. Lack of interest in sex is a major symptom of depression and can become a cycle in which the lack of interest causes depression which then triggers another round of impotence. If ignored long enough, this can cause a psychological impotence which may require therapy.

What Is Sensate Focus Therapy?

Masters and Johnson, in their world-famous institute for the study and treatment of sexual problems, developed some exercises that have been termed 'sensate focus therapy'.

In this type of therapy the couple learn to enjoy, slowly and progressively, non-intercourse-focused sexual activity. Couples learn they can caress each other and communicate physically and they are encouraged to do so without any expectations or requirements that this will end in intercourse or reaching orgasm for either one of them. During these exercises the couples are taught to express their sexual likes and dislikes, their needs and desires, something many of them have never done before, for fear of hurting their partner's feelings. They learn to mutually stimulate each other and engage in the kinds of stimulation that most excite their partner. The goal of these exercises is not to stimulate erection: it is to take the pressure off of HAVING to have an erection. It offers couples a way to please each other without the emotionally charged area of their dysfunctional sexual relationship. They are to please each other in a non-sexual way, to be together physically, to enjoy each other, to communicate in a way they perhaps have not experienced before. The goal of this therapy is to enable the couple to learn that erections can occur while being relaxed and playful with each other.

There are certainly other psychological treatments in cases of erectile dysfunction and the therapist will explore with the patient just what course might be the most beneficial.

What Can Be Done If Multiple Sclerosis Is Causing The Impotence?

Multiple sclerosis is a disease which causes plaques in the brain and on the spinal cord. The longer a man has MS, the more likely he is to be impotent. Although the impotence that results from MS tends to be progressive, many MS patients can successfully use penile injections or have a penile implant to restore their erectile function.

What Can Be Done If Spinal Cord Injury Is The Cause Of The Impotence?

The majority of spinal cord injuries are caused by compression fractures or dislocation of the vertebrae. Every year, there are serious cases of spinal cord injury resulting in impotence, from motor vehicle accidents, diving accidents and gunshot wounds. Seventy-five per cent of patients with spinal cord injuries lose some erectile function, usually because it interferes with the messages to the smooth muscle to relax.

Erections depend not only on signals passing back and forth between the penis and the spinal cord, but between the spinal cord and the brain. If the nerves between the spinal cord and the penis are intact, then direct stimulation of the penis will cause it to become erect. The more complete the neurologic injury, the greater the likelihood that potency will be adversely affected. An injury that involves a total severing of the spinal cord, resulting in complete paralysis and loss of sensation below the severance, is more likely to affect potency than a partial severing because when the paralysed man maintains some nerve function below the site of the injury he is likely to be able to maintain some erectile capability. Despite extensive paralysis, a surprisingly large number of paralysed men are capable of having and maintaining an erection, often with no electrical contact between the brain and the sex organs. These erections are brought about by making use of more primitive reflexes. These are triggered by stimulating the head of the penis with a vibrator or by touching specific trigger points on the inner thighs or under the testicles. In this case, the electrical signals take a short cut, from the sensitive nerves in the penis to the spine and from there back out again to the erection nerves controlling the erection.

Non-paralysed men can occasionally have similar short-circuits occur in the system from parallel circuits in adjacent organs such as the bladder. Signals from a full bladder can hop over to the erection nerves.

A battery-powered suppository which elicits an erection at the push of a remote-control button may be the answer for men who are chronically impotent from damage to the nerves that enervate erections. This suppository is designed to enhance neurologic reflexes and it stimulates nerves in the groin through the rectal wall. The suppository-like cylinder is inserted into the rectum just before sex and is activated by a tiny remote control mechanism. This process of anal stimulation makes it possible for men who might be incapable of intercourse to have an erection and possibly become a father by the in vitro fertilisation process with their sperm so gathered.

Those men who are incapable of erection of any kind can find the loss of sex devastating. However, with the help of a skilful therapist and an understanding sexual partner they can learn to refocus on a new erogenous zone. Some other area of the body can be eroticised by work with a therapist in a type of sensate focus therapy and the paralysed man can discover a new type of sex life which couples find satisfying and rewarding for both partners.

What Can Be Done When Failure To Store Is Causing The Impotence?

If the penis fills with blood, but won't store it, the problem is not with the arteries. If the arteries are working, pumping blood into the penis, the tissues of the erectile chambers must expand sufficiently to press up against the veins and compress them so that they will close off. It may be that the erectile tissue has lost elasticity.

This scarring or loss of elasticity results from the same things that damage the walls of the arteries. Two possible treatments are *venous ligation* and *crural plication*.

What Is Venous Ligation?

Venous ligation is vascular surgery that involves tying off or removing the veins that are causing excessive drainage of blood away from the erection chambers. In this procedure, the major veins draining the cavernosal veins are tied off, a vein known as the dorsal vein is removed and the remaining veins which drain the penis are left intact. It is important that the surgeon locate any and all of the leaking veins and that leakage must be mild. In men with moderate to severe leakage, surgical results will only be of temporary help. In such cases, if they cannot be successfully tied off then the inflow of the blood is improved by a combination of the venous ligation and revascularisation – the arterial bypass. The purpose of this surgery is to decrease blood drainage and thereby improve blood storage during erection. Younger men with fewer areas of storage abnormalities, men who do not have widespread venous problems, have a greater success rate for this type of surgery, which is successful in 28 per cent to 73 per cent of cases.

What Is Crural Plication?

Crural plication is the surgical tightening of the tissue that surrounds the erectile chambers so that it will compress the veins with the result that they will now close sufficiently to keep the blood in the penis. This tuck of the hidden portions of the penis is often performed simultaneously with the venous ligation. This is sometimes done when the venous leakage is severe enough to suggest that a ligation would be unlikely to take care of the problem of storage completely.

What Are The Advantages Of These Combination Surgeries?

A group of those who had either the outflow corrected, the bypass or both procedures done simultaneously were studied.

Of this group, the ones with the combination surgeries had the most success; 70 per cent were able to resume unassisted intercourse. Others were now able to benefit from injection-assisted erections and almost all felt satisfied that they had made some improvement in their erectile abilities.

What Are The Disadvantages Of These Combination Surgeries?

There is a potential loss of sensation in the penis in a small percentage of the cases, depending on the severity of the problem before surgery.

Most surgeons will not consider men over the age of 55 for these surgeries as they are seldom as successful as they are on younger men. The best candidates are men who are physically fit, non-smokers and with normal cholesterol levels. Surgeons may require men desiring these surgeries to quit smoking, undertake an exercise programme and a diet to control their cholesterol levels prior to their agreeing to perform this surgery.

Leaks may recur and require additional surgery.

What Other Options Are There For Venous Difficulties?

Sex therapy can be helpful, as well as vacuum constriction devices, penile injections and penile implants.

What Is A Vacuum Pump Or An External Assistance Device?

These devices consist of three parts - a hollow tube into which the penis is inserted, a hand-activated pump and a constriction band. The pubic area is lubricated and lubricant is placed at the lip of the cylinder where it meets the body to create a good seal. The pump is tugged a few times to generate a negative pressure. This causes blood to be sucked into the spongy tissues of the erectile chambers, creating an artificially-induced erection. Even men with arterial blockages find that the suction will pull the necessary blood into the penis. A sliding flexible rubber construction band is slipped onto the penis when the vacuum chamber is removed to keep the blood in place in the penis. Although the erection is not as firm as one that is naturally induced, it is rigid enough for intercourse. The constricting band should be left on no longer than 30 minutes. Sometimes there is difficulty with ejaculation because the constricting elastic band around the penis blocks the urethra and occasionally there is pain, bruising or swelling from the excessive negative pressure applied to the penis. Vacuum pumps are not recommended for men who suffer from bleeding disorders, spinal cord tumours, sickle-cell anaemia or recurrent priapism.

What Are The Advantages Of A Vacuum Pump Device?

These pumps are good for men who suffer from diabetes, medication-induced impotence, psychological impotence and others where both the blood flow system and the nerves are damaged from disease. They are non-invasive, inexpensive and temporary and there does not seem to be any limit on how often they can be used. They are a good solution for men who are only occasionally impotent or who have erections that are too flaccid for insertion.

What Are The Disadvantages Of Vacuum Pump Devices?

The man creating an erection with this device will never have an erection as firm as a natural erection, the penis tends to be wobbly at the base and the constriction ring cannot be left on for any longer than 30 minutes at a time. If left on longer it can create further problems, just as if it were a tourniquet.

The use of the pump interrupts the spontaneity of love-making. Without an understanding partner the man would need to excuse himself in order to create the erection. This device also requires some dexterity and time to apply, create the vacuum, apply the constriction ring before intercourse. For some couples, such as those where the man has MS, it might be possible for the partner to become a willing assistant in the use of the pump.

What Is Injection Therapy?

Several injectable drugs have proven effective in generating erections. If the physician decides that injections are appropriate, the patient is given a test injection in the physician's office. A small tourniquet is placed around the penis. The site on the side of the penis is sterilised and a test dose of the drug is administered. A very small-gauge needle is used and most men are surprised at how painless it is; the thought is more painful than the reality. This induced erection usually lasts from 90 minutes to 3 hours. If the erection doesn't subside then on its own, the patient must return to the physician immediately where another drug is given to remove the erection. If this test is successful, the patient will be taught to inject himself for subsequent erections.

What Is Papaverine?

Papaverine is a drug that works directly on the smooth tissues of the penis, relaxing both the arterial walls and the lacunar spaces within the erectile chambers. This allows them to fill with blood until they completely fill the casing that encloses the erectile chambers. This drug is not to be used more than once in 24 hours or more than three times in a given week. A lifetime limit of 500 injections is recommended for penile injection therapy for erections. However, this will extend a man's sexual life for quite a while and hopefully, medical science will advance so that there will be some other method of administration by that time.

What Is Phentolamine?

Phentolamine is an alpha blocker that prevents the sympathetic nervous system from shutting down the blood flow to the erectile tissue. It is usually given in a combination injection with papaverine in a ratio of 70 per cent papaverine to 30 per cent phentolamine. Used together, they increase the effectiveness of each other. More than 80 per cent of the men for whom injection therapy is suitable are able to achieve successful penetration.

What Is Prostaglandin E-1?

Prostaglandin E-1 is a naturally occurring substance important in the body's inflammatory response. While 90 per cent of the men with psychogenic and neurogenic impotence have responded favourably to the combination of papaverine/phentolamine injections, many patients with vasculogenic impotence fail to respond at all. Erections with prostaglandin E-1 occur approximately five minutes after injection and last about 20 to 60 minutes, compared with the one to three hours for papaverine. Many urologists now combine all three drugs.

What Is The Advantage Of The Three Drugs Treatment?

For years men have been aided in achieving erection by being injected with either papaverine, prostaglandin E-1 or a combination of papaverine and phentolamine. All three treatments have side-effects and for some men prostaglandin E-1 causes pain during sex. But when doctors mix all three drugs they get great results with smaller doses and fewer side-effects. The current success rate with the combination is up to 80 per cent.

What Are The Advantages Of Injectable Drugs?

They are highly effective in creating an erection strong enough for intercourse and have a success rate of about 80 per cent. Response is almost immediate and they are effective across a broad range of impotence causes including: purely neurogenic impotence (diabetes, multiple sclerosis, radical prostatectomy), those with minimum arterial insufficiency and minimal venous leaks. This means they can be used by a large number of men and they can be self-administered. Some men may find that their sexual partners are willing to administer the injections, turning what might be an embarrassing experience into an affectionate display of support.

What Are The Disadvantages Of Injectable Drugs?

There can be slight pain, bruising or bleeding, at the site of injection, particularly if the man is unskilful in giving himself the injection.

Scarring can occur with long-term dosage and priapism may occur with incorrect dosages. There is a limit to how long and how frequently the injections can be used.

What Is Yohimbine?

Yohimbine hydrochloride is made from the bark of the West African Yohimbe tree.

It is one of the oldest aphrodisiacs known to Man and one of the few whose effects on potency have been scientifically confirmed and explained. It has ingredients that are both libido-stimulating and erection-enhancing. It is beneficial in about 50 per cent of all cases of impotence regardless of the cause. This herb is an alpha-andrenergic blocking agent and it is believed to increase parasympathetic activity, which results in increased blood inflow as well as decreased blood flow to and from the penis. It is also more selective than most alpha blockers: while it allows some vasodilation (necessary for blood to flow more freely to the penis), it also enhances the release of norepinephrine, a hormone that contributes to the flexibility of the penile smooth muscle. It has been shown that norepinephrine is essential to the production of an erection and the presence of extra norepinephrine is what is thought to improve the erectile function. Yohimbine should not be used by men who have poor cardiovascular systems because of its side-effects on blood pressure. There are indications that Yohimbine may be more effective in men with partial impotence or in those who have been impotent for only a brief period of time. Success rates of 80 per cent have been reported for men who have been impotent for less than two years.

What Is Yohimbe?

A great many varieties of Yohimbine are available. Yohimbe is a non-prescription variety of Yohimbine and is actually the name of the tree from which the Yohimbine hydrochloride is extracted. Yohimbe is sold through health food stores and by mail order through men's magazines and many men think that by buying this product they are actually getting Yohimbine. It may or may not have the same potency or even be the same herb. Anyone without a healthy cardiovascular system should see their physician before considering purchasing this product because of its side-effects on blood pressure. Only the prescription form is actually Yohimbine hydrochloride.

What Are The Advantages Of Yohimbine?

This herb is taken orally and is an ideal first treatment option for all forms of impotence. It is easy to take and should be one of the first steps in seeing whether or not the man needs further treatment.

What Are The Disadvantages Of Yohimbine?

Yohimbine is rather slow acting, sometimes taking as long as eight weeks to produce results. It is effective only 50 per cent of the time; in the other 50 per cent it has no erectile effects at all. There are some side-effects associated with taking this drug, including dizziness and occasional nausea, as well as an increase in blood pressure.

Can Nitroglycerin Be Used To Increase Erections?

Nitroglycerin is used in the treatment and prevention of angina, the pain of narrowed blood vessels to the heart. It expands small blood vessels and increases blood flow. If nitroglycerin gel is rubbed onto the penis before sexual activity, a firmer erection is produced. One of the problems with this use is that the sexual partner may develop headaches during sex when the nitroglycerin enters the partner's bloodstream (through contact with the drug on the penis) and disturbs the blood flow to the brain.

What About Using L-dopa For Increased Potency?

L-dopa, a drug used to treat Parkinson's disease, has been found to stimulate erections as it elevates the body's level of dopamine. This natural brain chemical increases sexual arousal and in a recent study in impotent males who were not suffering from Parkinson's disease, it had a 70 per cent success rate.

What Are The Options When None Of These Treatments Work?

The penile implant is the option of last resort. The reason for this is that implant surgery is irreversible. Once it has been implanted, the surgery causes considerable scarring and the man, even if he has the implant removed, will never be able to have a successful normal erection again. Implants should only be considered in the following situations: men for whom injections have failed to produce satisfactory results; men who are unable, for whatever reason, to inject themselves; men for whom all other therapies have proven unsatisfactory; and men who suffer irreversible erectile problems due to diabetes or kidney disease or whose potency has been affected by bladder or prostate cancer surgery.

Men who have penile implants report a 90 per cent satisfaction rate. This makes treatment by penile implant one of the most successful of all treatment options for patients with irreversible impotence.

How Many Kinds Of Penile Implants Are There?

Implants are divided into two major categories: non-hydraulic and hydraulic. There are a variety of models being produced by different manufacturers. They are constantly being improved as new materials become available and solutions to problems of malfunctions are found.

During the Second World War, physicians experimented with ways to restore potency to men injured in combat. The first implants were made of part of a rib or cartilage inserted into the penis. These experiments were not successful, as these structures were eventually reabsorbed by the patient's own body. Today's implants are made of silicone and polyurethane, materials that are not absorbed or rejected.

How Does The Non-hydraulic Implant Work?

These are the most simple of all implants, consisting of a pair of silicone rods surgically placed in the erectile chambers of the penis. They maintain the penis in a state of rigidity, appearing to be semi-erect at all times. Some models can be bent down at the base and others have a rod with a ball-in-socket structure, which allows it to be bent upward and downward, creating a more natural look and feel. Most of them have either a silver braided cord wire or stainless steel wire centre.

However, they never completely mimic a normal erection because the erectile chambers no longer fill with blood, the circumference of the penis does not change and the penile implant may be half an inch to an inch shorter in length. The glans does not swell as it would in a normal erection, as the glans is part of the spongy tissue and the implant ends at the end of the erectile chambers.

There is one model that has a switching mechanism that shortens an internal cable to pull segments of it together for erection and then lengthens the cables by allowing them to slide apart when the man wants the penis to be flaccid.

What Are The Benefits Of The Non-hydraulic Implant?

Since these implants have fewer parts, there is less chance that they will malfunction. The surgery to implant them is fairly uncomplicated and since there is no fluid as there is in the hydraulic type, there is also no possibility of any leakage.

What Are The Disadvantages Of The Non-hydraulic Implant?

Even though the penis can be bent down when not erect, it appears to be in a state of rigidity at all times, which can be difficult to conceal underneath some clothing. Men with large penises have more difficulty concealing this type of implant. Men with long penises may find that some implants don't provide adequate support or rigidity. This is something the surgeon will discuss prior to the implant surgery in the process of selecting the right implant for the patient.

Also, there is no increase in penile girth as there is with a normal erection and the penile length is slightly decreased. The glans will not become firm as in a normal erection and implant rods can shorten further from being gradually pushed back into the pelvic tissue.

How Do Hydraulic Implants Work?

Hydraulic implants closely mimic the look and feel of a normal erection. As body tissues are composed mostly of water, a penis implanted with a hydraulic device feels more normal to the touch than one with a non-hydraulic implant. However, due to their design they are more complex as well as more prone to mechanical failure.

What Is A One-piece Hydraulic Implant?

The one-piece hydraulic implant has its tubes implanted within the erectile chambers and uses a small pump located underneath the glans to transfer fluid to an inner cylinder. When this inner cylinder is filled, additional pumping pressurises the chamber. Then when the man wishes to return the penis to a non-erect state, a release valve is pressed, causing the inner cylinder partially to deflate and the device to lose its rigidity. Another type is inflated by transferring the fluid from an outside chamber to an inside chamber. Bending the device down causes it to deflate. The fluid is pre-filled at the factory. Each of the cylinders operates independently of the other, so that an adequate erection can be achieved with only one chamber pumped up. This is an advantage if one of the cylinders should leak.

What Are The Advantages And Disadvantages Of The One-piece Implant?

These implants are less complicated than multi-piece devices and therefore have fewer potential problems inherent in their design. The fluid-containing reservoirs are located entirely within the implants themselves, so the fluid capacity is somewhat smaller. The erections obtained with these units do not feel or appear as full and these implants are not suitable for men with thick penises. Only a limited amount of fluid can be transferred from one portion of the device to the other and the penis remains semi-erect at all times. This implant is a good choice for men with long thin penises.

What Are The Advantages And Disadvantages Of The Two-piece Implant?

Some combine a reservoir and pump in a single unit which is inserted in the scrotum. The implant is inflated by pressing on a valve at the far end of the penis. Fluid is then transferred from the inner chamber to the outer chamber to achieve erection. Because reservoir and pump are a single unit, this usually cuts down on reservoir capacity. The amount of fluid, approximately 20 to 25ml, is sufficient for a man with a small penis. With these two-piece units, the penis remains semi-erect as a small amount of the fluid will remain in the penile cylinders. Should a mechanical problem arise, usually the entire system must be removed and replaced.

What Are The Advantages And Disadvantages Of The Three-piece Implant?

These implants have cylinders that are triple-layered. The inner layer is made of silicone and contains the fluid. The middle layer, of expandable Dacron, permits uniform expansion of the cylinder and a thin outer silicone layer prevents the Dacron from adhering to the walls of the erectile chambers. These implants have a fluid reservoir capacity from 60 to 125ml, making them the most expandable of all the implants and producing the largest and firmest erection. The large reservoir is the reason the three-piece implant is the right choice for men with large penises. The pump is implanted in the scrotum between the testicles, while the fluid reservoir is placed in the pelvic region below the rectus muscle. When the man wants an erection, he pumps it from between his testicles and a single depression of the pump deflates it.

It is common to use an iodine-based contrast medium in the fluid of the three-piece implants to make it easier to detect any fluid leaks with X-ray. If the individual is allergic to iodine, then only a sterile saline solution is used.

These implants provide excellent support and rigidity, creating a realistic-looking and feeling erection. As the fluid can be evacuated completely, the penis takes on a normal, flaccid appearance after sex. This implant has a higher risk of malfunction because it has more parts and occasional leakages have been reported. It may require more manual dexterity than other implants and may be unsuitable for men with neurological dysfunction. The glans never enlarges as with a normal erection and it is not recommended for patients who have extensive scarring in the pelvic area.

What Type Of Surgery Is Required For Implants?

As a general rule, surgery is done under general anaesthesia. No tissue is removed and very little blood is lost. The surgical incision may be made at several different locations on the penis, the pubis and the perineum, depending on the type of implant and the preference of the surgeon. The surgery may last from one to four hours, depending on the complexity of the model chosen. The patient can expect local discomfort for four to six weeks. The body reacts to the implants by encasing them in a thin layer of scar tissue, a perfectly naturally physiological response to something foreign being placed in the body.

Sex is avoided for at least a month. The penis is kept up against the abdomen while it heals. This is to safeguard against extensive scarring, so that the scarring around the implant will be uniform and not distort the surrounding tissue. Distortion of the tissue by improper scarring could mean that the implant would bend and fail to operate properly. Also, if scar tissue is allowed to form around a partially-full reservoir, the reservoir may never be able to expand sufficiently to hold the full volume of fluid in the system. Waiting two or four weeks for the scarring to complete allows the system to fill and empty completely. During this waiting period, the patient is taught how to activate and deactivate the implant, so that he is quite comfortable with the process when the time comes to use it. Most people can begin having intercourse within six weeks after surgery. This waiting period ensures complete healing and should allow pain-free intercourse.

How Many People Are Satisfied With Implants?

Approximately 90 per cent of implant recipients are satisfied and those who are not usually had unfulfillable and unrealistic expectations of what their implant would do and look like. Implants do not recreate normal erections. None of the implants increase the size or firmness of the head of the penis. After implant surgery, enlargement of the glans and urethra still depends on the sexual stimulation of intercourse. An erection from an implant may be as much as one or two inches shorter than previous natural erections. The circumference of the erection will also be affected by the implant. The three-piece implant increases the circumference of the penis, but most types don't. It is likely that the resulting implant circumference will be smaller than the man's previous natural erection.

How Do Partners React To Implants?

By the time a man decides to have an implant, his impotence is probably of at least six months' duration. A consideration of his sexual partner's thinking is important because once an implant is in place, the decision is irreversible. Usually, the partner is included in the steps leading up to the decision, has shared in the discussions and is knowledgeable about the procedure, the surgery and what can be anticipated with the results.

Occasionally, partners may have become accustomed to the non-sexual relationship, having found their own libido waning or having directed their energies elsewhere. The fears and expectations of both the patient and his partner need to be discussed very openly and freely in such cases and sex therapy is helpful both prior to and after the surgery. Sometimes the partner is disappointed in the appearance of the implanted penis and some couples find that their usual methods and positions need to be adjusted once the implant is in place. All these things need to be discussed with a professional sex therapist who can lead the couple towards better techniques and answer any questions before the surgery is done.

What Will An Implant Do For The Man's Interest In Sex?

If the lack of interest in sex was connected to the inability to have an erection, then the implant can solve that problem. If the difficulty was a decreased libido, then that is an entirely different matter and must be addressed either with hormonal treatment, should that be the difficulty, or with psychological counselling to address the other sexual problems that exist.

What Does The Penis With An Implant Feel Like?

Implants do not alter the sensations for the man. If the man could achieve orgasm and ejaculate before, he can expect to do so after the implant. Some men notice a change in their ability to urinate, but this is a rare complication. Some men notice that urination is less forceful or that they dribble slightly at the completion of urination. Neither of these things is painful.

The implanted penis does not feel the same to the sex partner as it did before, particularly in the semi-rigid rod type penis which does not feel the same as a normal flaccid penis. However, it should not be a problem, particularly if the partner has been involved in the implant process.

Can Implants Be Removed?

Implants can be removed but implant surgery causes injury and scarring of the penis's erectile tissue and removing the implant will not restore the erectile tissue to its state before the surgery. Most of the time, when implants are removed it is to replace them because of malfunctions.

Should Men Give Up Smoking And Drinking?

Men who really want to do some good for their erections should seriously consider giving up smoking, drinking and recreational drugs. Often men with long-standing erectile difficulties turn to alcohol or other drugs to escape the feelings associated with the dysfunction, but substance-abuse only compounds the problem and adds more destructive elements to the complications. Nicotine is a vasoconstrictor, which further closes down the small blood vessels which carry oxygenated nourishing blood to the penis. A smoker's peripheral arteries are harder, thicker and more clogged than those of non-smokers. By stopping smoking, men significantly improve their chances of remaining potent. Current research indicates that in some cases where no other medical conditions are present, stopping smoking can lead to the return of sexual function.

Alcohol, while it removes initial inhibitions, ultimately is destructive to blood vessels and adds to the problem of erectile dysfunction. Alcohol reduces the production of testosterone and heavy drinking impairs liver function. Since the liver is responsible for metabolising hormones, the reduced amount of hormones a long-term drinker produces may be insufficient to create a desire for intercourse. Normally the male body produces small amounts of the female hormone oestrogen and the liver destroys this oestrogen so there is no effect from it. With alcohol excess, the liver is no longer able to break down this oestrogen and this higher level of oestrogen causes a decrease in the production of testosterone and a consequent lowering of the sex drive.

Recreational drugs also remove inhibitions temporarily but soon compound the problem of the dysfunction. Cocaine, amphetamines and LSD all block serotonin in the brain and increase the levels of dopamine at first. Ultimately, more and more drugs are required to stimulate the same feelings and they begin to take their toll on other bodily functions which contribute to impotence. Eventually, the body responds to this imbalance in these brain chemicals with a variety of undesirable effects. There is a fine line between removing inhibitions and decreasing sexual functioning.

Will Exercise Increase Potency?

The more consistently an individual exercises, the lower the risk of a heart attack. Emotional and psychological well-being is also improved by regular exercise. In addition to toning the muscles so that you will look good and be attractive to a potential sexual partner, exercise lowers blood cholesterol and increases the level of endorphins, those brain chemicals that give you that feel-good feeling. A man who looks good and feels good has increased self-esteem which contributes to continued potency.

What Is The Major Preventive Measure To Retain Potency?

As we learn more about the way erections work and what affects them, we will begin to see more television programmes and more magazine and newspaper articles on the subject. That will be a very positive change because as long as men fail to realise the frequency of the problem and remain ignorant of the many solutions, they will have no idea that there is help available. Instead, uninformed, they will remain locked into the closed world of sexual dysfunction.

It is becoming clear that good health and open communications are necessary for men who want to retain their potency.

A low cholesterol, low fat, sugar-controlled, high-fibre diet can help avoid the vascular and nerve problems which are so prevalent in erectile dysfunction. Cigarettes, alcohol and other recreational drugs are time bombs on the road to continuing sexual power. Regular exercise is a must for any long-term love life. Just as a healthy lifestyle promotes good health, it promotes good loving and the stress that can sideline even the strongest athlete can also wreak havoc on the penis.

What Is The Future For The Treatment Of Erectile Difficulties?

Science is constantly looking for a breakthrough in the treatment of the diseases which cause impotence, as well as the problem of sexual dysfunction itself. As the ability to diagnose erectile problems gets better, so will the ability to treat those specific problems.

Some of the more promising work in diabetes management is as follows:

Genetics. Scientists are currently searching for the specific genes that produce faulty insulin receptors or other molecules critical for sugar's entry into cells. They are also looking for the factors that predispose some people to develop the destructive autoimmune response (wherein the cells become more and more resistant to insulin).

Islet (Beta) Cell Transplant. When researchers have implanted donated islet cells into kidney-transplant patients who are already taking immunosuppressant drugs, which inhibit rejection of foreign tissue, researchers are excited to find that they have reversed Type I diabetes for up to one year in some patients. They have also experimented with several approaches aimed at preventing rejection of these cells without using immunosuppressive agents. In one project, islet cells were encapsulated in tiny plastic tubes with holes big enough to release insulin but too small to allow immune cells to enter and destroy the islet cells. In another study, the cells were implanted in the thymus, a gland at the base of the neck in an attempt to trick the body into considering the transplanted cells as its own. So far, this technique has only been used in experimental animals, but it appears to hold some hope for the future.

Immunosuppressive Drugs. These drugs, which are used to suppress the immune systems of organ-transplant patients, are being tested on individuals who are genetically predisposed to Type I diabetes.

Low-dose Insulin. Researchers at the Joslin Diabetes centre in Boston are giving patients at risk for Type I diabetes daily low-dose injections of insulin and then hospitalising them every nine months for five days for interveinous insulin at a higher dosage. The treatment may help prevent the disease by allowing the pancreas to rest.

Infrared. A device which tests blood sugar levels by shining infrared light on the skin can now eliminate the finger stick for daily blood sugar testing. Delivering insulin through a nasal spray could eliminate injections.

The Chinese are currently treating impotence with *acupuncture*. Results on initial studies are encouraging and 63 per cent of the men in the study achieved erections.

The French have developed a *new penile injection device* about the size of a fountain pen and which has super thin needles. These needles are so thin they are barely felt during injection and inflict less scarring on penile tissue.

At present, doctors are using a process called *angiodilation* to unblock arteries by stretching them. Eventually it may be possible to stretch penile arteries with a miniature balloon to open up clogged areas and increase blood flow to the penis.

And it may soon be possible for doctors to administer irritating agents to the site of leaky veins. These *scarring agents* will cause benign scarring to block off leaky veins, instead of tying them off, as is done at present.

Hopefully, radiologists will be able to insert *miniature coils* via a catheter into those penile veins which are found to leak. These coils will adhere to the walls of the veins and block this excess blood leakage.

Researchers are working on *drugs that will make tissue more elastic,* improving its ability to expand and store blood during an erection, an achievement that could minimise the development of scar tissue.

Now that the highly effective female five-year birth control implant has gained acceptance, it may be possible to implant a similar device within the penis. This inconspicuous *implant would slowly release erection-stimulating medications* directly into the erection chambers, and could be refilled through direct injection into the implant itself.

Several different medications are currently available by patch, such as nicotine patches for cessation of smoking. It might be possible to provide the currently injectable *erection-causing drugs by patch,* which would mean that the current lifetime limit of 500 injections could be abandoned in view of the fact that the medication would be absorbed through the skin, directly into the penile structures. An American pharmaceutical manufacturer has developed an absorption enhancer which will allow some of these drugs to penetrate the skin but not enter the bloodstream, which will ensure that they will go where they are required and without affecting other body systems.

More *oral medications* will become available, to treat constricted arteries, to prevent blockages and to block the effects of body chemicals which interfere with erections. There are a number of pharmacological substances under investigation at the present by the major drug companies and hopefully some of them will become available soon.

Currently insulin is available by a *catheter and a pump implanted under the skin* which provides the diabetic with just the right amount of insulin at the right time. This method has possibilities for the future of the treatment of erectile difficulties, both with insulin and with erection-stimulating drugs.

Researchers are currently examining *Minoxydil,* the blood pressure medication which is also used to treat baldness. The side-effects of this medication are varied and it needs to be studied carefully before it can be recommended as a treatment for impotency.

Another area of research is in *atrial natriuretic peptides.* These natural hormones are generated by the heart to control blood pressure and several are currently being studied as alternatives to high blood pressure medications. Since many of the medications for high blood pressure cause impotence and these natural hormones do not, they may be an excellent alternative for many of the anti-hypertensive medications currently on the market.

A Danish firm is developing a new form of injectable treatment called *vasoactive intestinal peptide.* This peptide is the last neurotransmitter in the chain of sexual arousal. It is expected that it will be another injectable to relax the smooth-muscle tissue and decrease the outflow of blood from the erectile chambers.

A panel of experts convened by the National Institutes of Health in the USA has said that there are more effective sex therapies today than a decade ago for the treatment of impotence but access to them is hampered by the reluctance of both physicians and patients to discuss impotence. Accurate statistics on the extent of the problem are difficult to unearth because so many people are too embarrassed to discuss it. The panel urges that men should not believe the myth that impotence is inevitable and recommend that there be more overall public discussion of the problem, including public service announcements on radio and television and frequent community lectures. They further suggest that the term 'impotence' be discarded in favour of 'erectile dysfunction' because 'impotence' has the 'connotation of powerlessness'. The panel chairman said, "Impotence implies weakness. It is not a weakness at all."

Why Are Researchers Taking A New Look At An Ancient Remedy?

Researchers in the USA are studying a chemical extracted from celery that lowers blood pressure by relaxing the smooth muscles that line the blood vessels. They hope it will lead to a new treatment for hypertension free of the side-effects of impotence and dizziness that plague its current remedies. A small amount of the chemical extracted from celery, called *3-n-butyl phthalide,* lowered blood pressure 12 to 14 per cent and cholesterol by seven per cent. The amount was equal to that found in about four stalks of celery. Interestingly, celery and its oil have been used in Oriental folk medicine for centuries to treat circulatory disorders.

What Is The Possible Amazing Breakthrough Cure For Impotence?

Not too long ago *nitric oxide's* only known role was as an energy source for lowly bacteria, but that changed recently when scientists found nitric oxide all over the human body. Researchers found that a defect in the body's production or use of this gas called nitric oxide could be a major cause of impotence. Nitric oxide allows muscle tissue in the penis to relax so it can fill with blood and enlarge. This new research has finally helped explain one of the basic processes that takes place during an erection and may yet furnish further clues to smooth muscle relaxation in the penis. They think that it is possible that something goes wrong with nitric oxide in men who can't achieve erections. Nitric oxide is a component of smog and acid rain and it is produced in such tiny amounts for fractions of a second throughout the body that it has been very difficult to trace or examine.

It should not be confused with nitrous oxide – laughing gas, which is often used, mixed with oxygen, as a sedative to patients undergoing dental work.

These fleeting puffs of nitric oxide in the human body are an unstable gas that just lasts five seconds and appear to be absolutely essential for regulating blood vessels. It may prove to be one of the most powerful known biological substances in the human body and may point the way for the most exciting research yet on the cause and treatment of impotence. It is possible that with the unravelling of the role of nitric oxide that the problem of impotence will no longer exist.

There are so many exciting things occurring in medical research that there is hope of a new treatment which will be readily available, simple to perform and excitingly effective, for each and every man. Until that time, REMEMBER, AT THIS VERY MOMENT – 97 PER CENT OF MEN CAN BE TREATED OR CURED!

It is up to you.

GLOSSARY

alkaloids	basic substances in plants which are physiologically active.
adrenaline	a substance which is secreted by the adrenal glands and acts upon the smooth muscle, causing it to contract.
androgen	a group of hormones which are responsible for the development and maintenance of male secondary sex characteristics.
aphrodisiac	substance to create sexual desire and potency.
arteriography	an X-ray of the arteries, made by introducing dye into them.
arteriole	the smallest blood vessel in the circulatory system carrying blood away from the heart.
artery	a large vessel, under pressure that carries blood from the heart to various organs of the body.
atherosclerosis	a disease process whereby fatty deposits line the walls of the arteries.
autonomic nervous system	the part of the peripheral nervous system that regulates automatic functions such as breathing.
Ayuravedic	India's herbal tradition.
bypass surgery	a surgery used to go around a blockage in the artery, to increase blood flow.
cavernosography	an X-ray of the erectile chambers of the erect penis.
Celsus, Aulus	Roman encyclopaedist.
central nervous system	the system that controls the bodily functions – the brain and the spinal cord.
collagen	a protein tissue that is in bundles or interwoven fibres which strengthen the tissue.

corpus cavernosum (corpora cavernosa)	one of a pair of balloon-like erectile chambers of the penis.
corpus spongiosum	the portion of the penis that contains the urinary tube, conducting the urine to the outside of the body.
Cowper's gland	a gland at the base of the penis which excretes an oily lubricant.
crural plication	a surgical procedure for tightening tissue of the tunica.
crus (crura)	the back portion of the corpora cavernosa.
damiana	herb containing a mildly irritating oil.
DICC	a series of tests - dynamic infusion cavernosometry and cavernosography – for evaluating the ability of the penis to fill and store blood.
dita	tree with potent alkaloid, native to Southeast Asia.
dopamine	chemical messenger that increases stimulation of the nervous system.
endocrinologist	a physician who specialises in disorders of the hormones.
endothelium	a layer of cells that line the interior of blood cells or other tissue.
epididymis	the oblong body attached to the upper part of each testicle, containing the tubing of the vasa efferentia.
eunuch	castrated man.
fenugreek	potent herb of bitter oil and alkaloids.
foreskin	retractable covering of the glans.
flaccid	the absence of firmness in an erection.
ginkgo biloba	herb from a tree native to eastern China.
ginseng	herb containing chemicals which stimulate.
glans	the head of the penis
gotu kola	herb containing several alkaloids.
guarana	herb with a high caffeine content.

Hippocrates	Greek physician called the father of medicine.
iliac artery	the artery that supplies the blood to the pelvic area.
implant	an artificial device that will provide the rigidity necessary for intercourse.
impotence	the inability to achieve and maintain an erection of sufficient rigidity for intercourse to ejaculation.
initiation	the ability to signal the penis to fill with blood.
kava kava	herb of perennial shrub native to the South Pacific.
lacunar space	the specialised endothelium-lined space of the erectile tissue of the penis.
libido	sexual drive.
motor nerves	those nerves that transmit messages from the brain and the spinal cord to perform their function.
neuropathy	a disease process of the nerves whereby they do not respond properly to messages from the brain.
neurotransmitter	a chemical released by the nerves that carries messages to other nerves or to muscles.
noraderenaline	an adrenaline-like substance secreted by both nerve cells and adrenal glands, which causes the smooth muscle to contract.
occluded	blocked.
papaverine	a drug used to induce an erection.
peripheral nervous system	the motor and sensory nerves which are outside the brain and spinal cord.
Peyronie's disease	a condition of the penis which is characterised by curvature at erection.
phentolamine	a drug used to induce an erection.

plaque	hard nodules caused by fatty deposits or by scarring.
potency	the ability to sustain an erection of sufficient firmness for intercourse to ejaculation.
priapism	a prolonged erection without sexual desire. Priapus – the Greek god of crops and herds, symbolic of sexuality.
prostaglandin E-1	a drug used to induce an erection.
prostate	the gland which surrounds the neck of the bladder and the urethra.
Saint Valentine	patron saint of lovers.
sarsaparilla	sweet tasting root of climbing vine native to tropical America.
seminal vesicle	a small sack that produces the protective medium for the semen.
sensate focus	a psychological treatment used to reduce anxiety and restore pleasure to sexual partners.
sensory nerves	nerves that transmit messages from the skin and other organs to the spinal cord and brain.
serotonin	chemical messenger that reduces stimulation of the nervous system.
smooth muscle	one of the three types of muscle in the body.
Spanish fly	powder of the beetle cantharis.
testosterone	the male hormone which is responsible for the development of the secondary male characteristics as well as the libido.
tunica albuginea	the fibrous sheath that surrounds the erectile chambers of the penis.
urethra	a canal that carries both semen and urine to the outside of the body.
urologist	a physician who specialises in the genito-urinary system.

vas deferens	the excretory duct from the testicle.
vein	a blood vessel that conducts blood, usually under low pressure, to the heart.